MISFITS *FURTHER* ABROAD

....

PEOPLE AND ADVENTURES AROUND THE WORLD

MARTINE ROBINSON BEACHBOARD

Livingwell Publishing

TAOS, NEW MEXICO, USA

Copyright © 2026 Martine Robinson Beachboard
All rights reserved.
No part of this publication may be reproduced, distributed, or transmitted in any form or by any means, including photocopying, recording, or other electronic or mechanical methods, without the prior written permission of the publisher, except in the case of brief quotations embodied in critical reviews and certain other noncommercial uses permitted by U.S. copyright law. For permission requests, contact the publisher, addressed:

Livingwell Publishing. ATTN: Permissions Coordinator
1417 Santa Cruz Road, Taos, New Mexico 87571 USA
www.livingwellpublishing.com

Book Cover by Natalia Larguier

"DK Eyewitness Travel Guides" published by Dorling Kindersley. Penguin Random House, London, UK.
"Gender Equality: At the Centre of IT... and Beyond" © Kosovo Women's Network (2024).
"Ghostbusters" screenplay written by Dan Aykroyd and Harold Ramis. Columbia Pictures (1984).
"Gone with the Wind" screenplay by screenwriter Sidney Howard and producer David O. Selznick. Metro-Goldwyn-Mayer (1939). Novel written by Margaret Mitchell, The Macmillan Company (1936).
"Harry Potter and the Sorcerer's Stone" written by J.K. Rowling. Scholastic. (1997).
"HeroRATS: Rats Who Save Lives" by Gabrielle Fimbres. Published by Learning A-Z (2022).
"I Have Confidence" by Rodgers & Hammerstein; "The Sound of Music." Twentieth Century Fox (1965).
"In the Shadows: A Gender Analysis of Informal Work in Kosovo" © Kosovo Women's Network (2024).
"Star Trek IV: The Voyage Home" screenplay by Harve Bennett and Nicholas Meyer. Story by Steve Meerson and Peter Krikes. Directed by Leonard Nimoy. Produced by Harve Bennett. Paramount Pictures (1986).
"The Goonies" screenwriters: Chris Columbus and Steven Spielberg. Directed by Richard Donner. Warner Bros. (1985).
"The Man Who Knew Too Much" screenplay by John Michael Hayes. Directed by Alfred Hitchcock. USA: Paramount Pictures (1956).
"The Raiders March" composed by John Williams, EMI and Warner/Chappell Music. Featured in "Raiders of the Lost Ark" screenplay directed by Steven Spielberg, written by Lawrence Kasdan (story by George Lucas and Philip Kaufman). Lucasfilm Ltd./Disney (1981).

For privacy reasons, names and some locations and dates have been changed.

Misfits *Further* Abroad: People and Adventures Around the World /
Martine Robinson Beachboard – 1st ed.
ISBN (Paperback Edition) 979-8-9915191-4-4
ISBN (Hardback Edition) 979-8-9915191-6-8
ISBN (eBook) 979-8-9915191-5-1
Library of Congress Control Number: 2025926374

INSIDE

WE SEEK ADVENTURE
POMPEII

EGYPT

MOROCCO

UNITED ARAB EMIRATES

VIETNAM

INDIA

PAKISTAN

JORDAN

TURKEY

KOSOVO

THE ADVENTUROUS SEEK US
VIETNAM

NEPAL

RUSSIA

***

GLOSSARY

MAP

DISCUSSION GUIDE

AUTHOR'S BIOGRAPHY

To John, my institutional memory, who's been honored in multiple countries by gifts of headgear too small for his American head. And to the memory of Thanh Van, who allowed me to edit her book, and the memory of MaryJo, who lived the book we had hoped to write together.

ACKNOWLEDGMENTS

Thank you for hours of assistance and years of friendship, Patricia Herrewig, James Herrewig, and Daniel Mintie.

INTRODUCTION

In a previous account, the Misfit took on Europe. That story is related in *Misfits Abroad: Adventures in Love, Language, and Foreign Lands*. Now she embarks on adventures farther abroad and further afield. The vignettes presented here introduce people and places encountered when she ventured into Asia and parts of the African continent. These travels taught her to appreciate religions, landscapes, cuisines, and architecture on the other side of the world. It is the author's hope that these stories will enrich readers' lives too.

This book is nonfiction, but it is not social-science research or a documentary. It offers anecdotes from the writer's experiences and observations. No one instance is intended to be broadly representative of any culture or group.

PREFACE

FACES OF FEAR

The only thing we have to fear is... everything!
(with apologies to Franklin D. Roosevelt)

An anxious person sees danger everywhere.
On a plane. In a boat.
In the dark. On a mountainside.
On Italian roads or the island of Rhodes.

Fear of Flights

My first-ever flight was on a little Cessna, and I was seated next to an off-duty pilot. Eager to do my part to keep the craft aloft, I tightened my seatbelt snugly and pulled up on the armrests. Shut the window shade. That helps, right? Every equipment rattle, heat bump, banking, revving, slowing down, or slight descent evoked a startled gasp from me.

"You're the most nervous passenger I've ever seen," my seatmate observed.

"That's probably true," I acknowledged. "Anyone more nervous wouldn't get on the plane at all."

Fear of Deep Water

The swimming gear in my husband's bag had been speaking to him since we'd arrived in Greece. An afternoon at the beach was not on the cruise agenda, but before our shore excursion at Rhodes, he consulted a map and figured out where he could put his snorkeling paraphernalia to good use. On the ride to Lindos, he spotted his chosen site and pointed it out to the bus driver. After guided temple tours, we caught the bus back northward. Before we reached Rhodes, John leapt up and reminded the driver where to stop.

"We'll catch a ride back," he told the tour guide.

We walked down on the sand to a small cove; the only other people there were Greek fishermen in weathered little boats. With a book, water bottle, and beach towel, I stretched out to watch and wait. "Sunscreen!" I called out. He was already waist deep in the waves, and besides he'd only be out there for twenty minutes.

At first it was fun to watch him swimming, floating face down with a snorkel mask and fins. What sorts of wonders were under that azure surface? The sunshine was dazzlingly bright, but I could read a bit and glance up to check on him. He was getting smaller and smaller. Floating northward.

The next time I looked up from my paperback, he was out of sight. The waves and his wanderlust had carried him around a promontory. That's OK; he'll turn back soon. Won't he?

I went back to reading. Tried to concentrate.

Has it been an hour?

The winds picked up; the sun was gliding closer toward the horizon.

Yes, it had been an hour.

Maybe the current was too strong. Maybe he got hit by a motorboat. Maybe he got a muscle cramp and drowned. Maybe I'm stranded on this isolated shore with a few rugged strangers and night coming on.

An hour and a half.

By this time I had worked myself into such a panic, I ran and got sick in the bathroom. More like an outhouse.

For a while I paced back and forth along the beach. Fishermen offered to take me out on the water to look for my partner. As I was weighing this option, a dripping wet, lobster-red, broadly smiling man strode across the sand from the direction of Rhodes.

I couldn't decide whether to be more angry or more relieved. The fishermen smiled and waved. We trekked back to the road to hitch a ride.

By bedtime John was moaning in pain from the brutal sunburn on his back. As my Czech grandmother might have said, he paid for his fun.

Fear of Shallow Water

Uncle Homer loved fishing. In the summer our families would vacation in the White Mountains of Arizona, and we would all go out on Bartlett Lake in a fourteen-foot aluminum rowboat. My father would put a fishing pole in my five-year-old hands, and I was supposed to let one of the grownups know if I felt anything dragging at the line. When something did tug, I was terrified it was a rainbow trout so huge it would pull *me* over the side of the boat rather than the other way around.

The biggest thing that ever snagged my hook was a big, slimy glop of seaweed.

Never a decent swimmer, in spite of instruction from several pros, I continued to fear any body of water larger than a municipal pool. Especially water I couldn't see through. Thus, kayaking in Cancun was not going to be my favorite part of our ecotourism outing. If I didn't feel safe in a flat-bottomed rowboat, I was sure to find it a challenge even to get situated in a watercraft with a V-shaped hull.

Heading out in pairs, each kayak team was expected to navigate through the Nichupté Lagoon, a system of narrow channels that wound through mangrove forests connecting seven bodies of water.

Having neither strength nor coordination, I was a poor paddling partner. We couldn't propel evenly or in unison. I had no understanding of the dynamics involved in turning a craft in water. Consequently, we kept banging into the banks of the lagoon inlets with their seagrass lining.

"Not so fast!" I cried. "Why are we turning in circles?"

Now I was paying more attention to my lifejacket than my paddle.

"We're going to tip over!" I shrieked more than once. "How do we steady this thing?"

John was probably quite frustrated by the time we exited the second channel, but he replied calmly.

"You could stand up," he said.

"Stand up? Are you crazy? Then we'll tip over for sure!"

The rest of our little sailing adventure was spent trying to make sure we got to the other side of the lake in time to join the rest of our tour group.

Safely back on land, I turned to John: "What did you mean, I should stand up?"

"I meant," he replied evenly, "that you weren't going to drown, because the water was so shallow you could have stood up and never been in over your head."

Fear of Heights

A road in the Dolomites of Italy. Jagged white peaks and deep valleys. The cliffside route downhill was peppered with tight switchbacks. John drove. I was tense and cringing the whole way down. Clutching the car ceiling's grab-handles. "Please slow down. Please slow down. I don't care how many speeding motorists are behind us. Let them wait!" We were both going to be miserable all day long if something didn't change.

On the shore of a lake near the bottom of the pass was a small shop; John went in and bought the only tranquilizer available. Grappa. *This ought to relax her a little.*

Or a lot. I sipped it like wine. No immediate effect other than a burning throat, so I swigged some more. The reaction was delayed but not unpleasant. I began to relax, and soon I felt downright normal. For the remaining curves along our route that afternoon, I was a kid on a roller coaster.

Whee!

Such self-medicating would not be advisable while hiking, so I got no chemical relief on my next acrophobic adventure.

John could hardly wait to climb in the Dolomites. Deep green forests. Steep white rock faces. Plunging gorges.

We packed water and a snack, donned hiking boots, grabbed a map, and set out from a comfortable and picturesque chalet. The sky was a clear, clean blue following storms that had recently ripped through the valley.

We'd not gone long before our mountainside trail seemed to differ from the map. Shouldn't we have gone off to the right fairly early on?

There was no side path in sight, just a sheer drop-off on the right, and mountainside on the left. We kept climbing.

Now there was a ski lift over our heads. Not running. Off season. The dirt beneath our feet became gravel. Scree. My rugged shoe soles began slipping backward. And sideways toward the edge of the drop-off. If it's this hard to climb up, how will I maintain control on the descent?

Anxiety set in. *I can't do this.* I was unwilling to move farther up and afraid to start back down.

It will get better, my trekking companion assured me. If we don't find our turn-off, we'll take a later one, John said. Or we'll follow the chairlift route to the top of the mountain.

But there was no later trail branch. Just another sharp cliff straight ahead of us. Two routes diverged: The valley floor dropped sharply, and the lift cables rose overhead. A vast crevasse stood between us and the ski lift terminal.

We had to go back: John hiking down, me scooting on my dungareed derrière, hugging the mountain side of the scree slope. The clamber was exhausting physically and emotionally. It left me shaky.

After we returned to our hotel and I regained my wits, another hiker told us that recent torrents had completely washed out our trail and the sign that used to mark it. There was no way up or down that mountain other than the ski lift that soared across the gap.

Sometimes your fear is not irrational.

◦❧◦

IF THEY COULD SEE ME NOW

"I'm glad Mother's dead. I'm glad she's dead so she can't see me...."
~Scarlett O'Hara, *Gone with the Wind*

Scarcely a day goes by that I don't miss my parents and regret that they're not here to talk to, consult with, share with, say thank you to. Yet...

Would I have traveled to Pakistan if my father had known? Toured mosques and markets in Istanbul if my mother had been alive to worry about me? Flown into Cabo San Lucas alone at midnight to drive through the desert for a wedding, if my parents were sitting by the phone waiting to hear from me?

For all my fears and misgivings, I still wanted to go places. Or at least, to be in other places, preferably arriving by the Star Trek "beam me up" method. Once I'd grown accustomed to thirty-some countries in Europe, it seemed like time to press outward again, beyond my new comfort zone, and to venture further abroad. To lands where I didn't speak the language, where no one looked like me, and where I couldn't blend into the crowd.

The most worrisome thing I'd done during my youth was joyride down at the San Pedro River in girlfriends' cars or speed on the backs of boys' motorcycles. Now here I was, like the novice Sister Maria von Trapp, seeking adventure and the courage to do things I'd not previously dared.

WE SEEK ADVENTURE

POMPEII

TWO CANINES AT VESUVIUS

Ever mindful of an opportunity to extend a subsidized trip, my husband and I did some touring after presenting an academic paper on critical-thinking pedagogy at a conference in Cassino, Italy. There we visited the Abbey of Montecassino. In nearby Caserta, we toured the palace. Later we would hike on the Amalfi Coast, where large, aromatic lemons are hand-harvested on steep mountainsides. Most of all, I was bursting with enthusiasm to take the train to Pompeii, the ancient Roman city buried by the eruption of Mount Vesuvius.

This tragically famous archaeological site had intrigued me since a high school English class required the reading of a short story about a blind boy whose dog was buried in a flash of ash in AD 79. The tale revolved around archaeologists finding the remains of a dog with a fossilized raisin cookie in its mouth. Though the residents of Pompeii surely felt early rumblings from nearby Mount Vesuvius, thousands did not flee in time to survive. The scientists in the fictional story found it odd that an animal would be carrying food from a bakery instead of sheltering itself: "I wonder what made him want it at such a moment."

If I ever got from my little Arizona town to the world's largest excavated archaeological site, which of the relics from 1,900 years earlier would most intrigue me?

After three hours on trains with our convention colleagues, we approached the Archaeological Park of Pompeii. The visit would take me back thirty years to a classroom in the desert. Its artifacts would take us back to findings uncovered as early as 1748.

Moments after John and I reach the entrance and acquire our tickets, a torrent of rain sends tourists over to hastily set up vendor displays of umbrellas and thin plastic ponchos. As soon as everyone in the crowd has bought one or the other, the downpour stops.

Just inside the entrance, we are greeted by our group's prearranged tour guide.

The woman is friendly, well spoken, and well schooled.

Couldn't she make her introduction while standing in front of the Forum?

She offers an overview of Vesuvius geology.

I want to go walk in the rubble.

She describes daily life from first-century Rome.

I want to find a fossilized bakery.

She shares details about the Sanctuary of Apollo and Temple of Venus.

I should be strolling past remnants of markets.

She explains the significance of the Stabian Baths.

Let me go step around puddles created by the recent rain.

She discusses the condition of the various frescoes.

Can't she walk us over to see these paintings in the House of the Tragic Poet?

I start edging my way toward the periphery of the group.

This guide is passionate about her subject. She can answer a multitude of questions. Our group is made up of professors, so there are many questions, some of them comments or elaborations masquerading as questions.

Hundreds of acres of ruins and relics are begging to be walked through. Yet she keeps talking. We are standing just inside the entrance but still too far from the excavations to see anything of the recommended sites, let alone a bakery with a dead dog inside.

By this time, I'm jumping out of my skin. *Could she please wind up her speech now? Maybe give us brochures to read later? Could she at least talk while walking, getting us closer to what we have come to see? A UNESCO World Heritage Site.*

We have been warned that if we miss returning with the group, we'll be on our own to get back to Cassino. Finally, with an apologetic glance toward the conference director, I make a run for it.

Before the afternoon is over, I manage to see the Amphitheater and baths and brothels and representations of the dead. I've viewed fossils and skeletons and mummies before, but only in Pompeii have I seen "negative skeletons." People's shapes formed bubbles in the pumice: three-dimensional outlines of the void left by vaporized bodies. The iconic "remains" that are on display are casts, created by pouring plaster into the hollow voids left behind after victims decomposed in the ash. Their dying positions reflect horror and human vulnerability.

Finally someone shows me the way to a fabulous mosaic in the entryway of a wealthy man's home. In tiny, contrasting tiles, it has a remarkably intact double border around an image of a black dog and the Latin words, *"Cave canem."*

Beware of the dog.

EGYPT

FASCINATED BY THE SPHINX

"I'd never seen anyone as white as you," the woman said.

The observation was not about my race or social perspective. It was about my health. Several of us intrepid travelers to Egypt had promised to keep in touch after the Christmas-holiday trip, but when I called this Department of Defense school teacher, it took her a moment to remember who I was.

I described my husband, then added, "You didn't see a lot of me. I got really sick and hardly left our cabin."

"Oh! You're the one. Your husband carried you through the Luxor airport. You were pale as death. How are you doing now?"

Obviously, I had survived, although a week in Egypt had sapped some of the lifeblood out of me.

Food poisoning rendered me unconscious most of the week. If I was upright, I fainted dead away. Sometimes on the bathroom floor. Which may explain the parasites that manifested a couple of weeks later. How did this happen? I'd been so careful. Hardly eaten anything. I'd used the recommended vodka to brush my teeth. What else could I do? Or not do?

This was not a luxury cruise, our American Express travel agent had advised. No, it sure as heck wasn't. That fact was substantiated before our EgyptAir craft departed from the Frankfurt tarmac. John and I had barely buckled our seatbelts when a teenaged girl behind us let out a shriek. Skittering across the back of her seat was a lively, well fed cockroach.

We arrived in Cairo. Fascinating, overflowing with culture and history. One of the largest cities in Africa, it had twelve million people at that time. It smelled crowded, the air gray and oppressive from fumes. It didn't take long before everything – your clothes, your luggage, your body fluids – had the same odor. Our lodging was on one edge of the city in a modest motel-like resort. A little campus of several buildings. It was balmy so we could walk outdoors between the row of guest rooms, the gift shop, and the dining room.

Breakfast featured ample baskets of breads. Cooked tomatoes. A stainless-steel chafing dish with a big batch of what looked like refried pinto beans seemed safe enough. Except for the decorative garnish of two raw eggs plopped on top. *I'm going to serve myself from the side of the pan to avoid those guys.* I eschewed salads and dairy products. Platters of colorful produce I also thought I should avoid. Other dishes looked enticing, but I was warned and wary, so I didn't eat much. I didn't even do my usual trick of saving some bread or surreptitiously making a sandwich for later. If I got hungry, I'd tuck into a package of Fig Newtons from my pack.

The first couple of days were a wish come true for a small-town American gal. Egypt had always been on my father's dream list. He was fascinated by the image of the Great Sphinx, a 240-foot-long lion with a human head. Dad's enthusiasm inspired me to want to see this wonder along with the pyramids and all the rest. Not that he expressly encouraged me to make the trip; in fact, he was convinced I would catch something deadly if I did.

After being exposed to countless schoolbook stories about the land called the Gift of the Nile, I couldn't wait to see a real-life mummy. So to speak. Off we went to the National Museum of Egyptian Civilization. I'd always heard that the mummies were remarkably well preserved. In my naïve mind, that meant something resembling a corpse you might see in a casket at a funeral. This shrunken little guy did still have skin on his bones, but it was black and wizened.

Leaving Cairo, we rode past men on foot leading donkeys heavy-laden with goods destined for market. To witness such scenes is to slip out of yourself and into the pages of a children's Bible storybook. These are not actors putting on a show; this is their authentic life. This is what an excursion can do: take you not just to another place but to another time.

At Giza, we crawled into a dusty, claustrophobic one-way tunnel in a pyramid. The best part was the privilege of being inside a structure 4,500 years old.

Going underground at the Saqqara necropolis was a moving experience. The burial *mastabas* were gracefully decorated with designs retaining their color better than some frescoes I've seen in French cathedrals. If you're impressed now, wait until you visit the Valley of the Queens, other travelers told me.

One day the motorcoach dropped us all off at the huge open bazaar Khan el-Khalili. Don't get lost, the tour guide warned. There's another parking lot just like this one on the other side. Come back here on time, or we'll leave without you. Those were her directions. Then she was gone. The renowned Paris flea market doesn't particularly excite me, but put me at an outdoor bazaar in Asia or the Middle East, and I'm transported. Every stall's intense colors and overpowering smells tingle my nerves. Spice barrels. Dried fruits. Leather goods and textiles. Earthen crockery and metal pots. Clothing and sandals. Baskets, trinkets, and figurines. All of it calls to me, not necessarily to buy but to experience. This is unfortunate for the salesmen, who are not there for my entertainment and picture-taking but to earn a living.

A colleague had requested we bring her some perfume, so we decided to work on that errand first. This seemingly modest request consumed most of our available afternoon. We didn't just walk up to a tent-covered booth and grab some random pretty bottle. We got snared into a stifling, cramped storefront for an explanation and a lecture about where these special colognes came from. Then we had to drink tea. *No, thank you, I already need to use a restroom now.* These women were graciously hosting us like guests, and all the while I was yearning to escape into the market morass. Ah, but one was obliged to drink the tea. Not just any tea: tea with frankincense. *Hold the myrrh, please.*

Finally, our purchase was wrapped in paper and string, and we emerged into the sunshine. Again the wild assortment of goods called to me. Their hawkers literally so. Alas, so did my kidneys, and there was no potty on the motorcoach, so we started asking strangers where the facilities were. If Scarlet O'Hara had the smallest waistline in three counties, I had the smallest bladder in three countries. For a tip of a few *piastres*, a man wearing a *dishdasha* led me across the lot to the opposite edge of the souk. Stalls with porcelain foot pads. Do you stand? Squat? Position your face or back toward the wall? Whatever. Just go. *How do you spell relief?*

Now it was time to push our way back through the steaming maze of humanity and bartered wares to the designated parking lot. Concern over missing our ride back to the hotel was more compelling than the vending stalls.

We need not have worried. Others in our party arrived later than we. Notably a college kid who had bought a dirty old camel saddle. No room for that on the tour bus; it would have to go underneath, in the luggage compartment. How was he going to get this nasty-looking thing through customs? He was determined: *It's mine, and I'm keeping it.* Wouldn't his mother be thrilled with that thing if he did manage to get it home?

One of my goals when I'm abroad is to be inconspicuous. That's harder in some places than others. Westerners could not escape notice in the capital city. When our motorcoach drove us for an overview tour, where the air was thick with the smell of exhaust, it passed older buses filled with children who waved and called out greetings to us. Their vehicles were worn and rusted, windows rolled down. When we got behind any of these buses, we recognized the Mercedes logos on the back. How long had it been since these particular specimens had left the Daimler-Benz plant south of Stuttgart?

Everywhere we went, walking on a sidewalk, visiting a temple, men extended their hands begging for *baksheesh*.

One middle-aged man, dressed in a worn-out cotton *thobe*, spied John's ballpoint pen and wanted it. It was the fat plastic type that had three slide levers on the sides to alternately extend three ink colors: red, blue, and black. Childlike, he began to work the mechanism and mark his dark skin with the different inks. I started to protest the man's petty thievery; John said to let him keep it. It was obviously giving him such pleasure.

A stop intended to satisfy the shopping cravings of wealthy travelers and enrich the local merchants – and probably the tour director and driver – was at a carpet factory. It was a school, we were told. The workers were young apprentices, learning skills that would help them get better jobs when they grew up.

I was getting sick by that time and felt too puny to leave the bus, but John came back for me, asking if I had any candy in my bag and urging me to go inside and see what he had seen. Beautiful little girls, about eight years of age, in thin cotton dresses, sat at backless stools working large looms. Their delicate fingers deftly wove the silk or woolen threads.

"*Bonbonla?*" they asked. John had offered them coins, since everyone on the street always wanted tips. A big-eyed girl in a pale-pink dress accepted the money with no enthusiasm.

"*Bonbonla? Bonbonla?*" she repeated. What does this mean, he asked the local tour guide. Candy, she replied. Like bonbon.

Sweets produced a broad, genuine smile that broke our hearts.

Ah! Any monetary gift would be taken by the boss the minute we left the factory, but the goodies she was allowed to enjoy for herself.

This was not a school. Not an internship. This was exploitation of tiny, nimble fingers. Hands that would not be productive and profitable in a few years. That's why no one older worked here.

I will *never* buy carpets made by children.

***

That was it for the on-land component of our adventure. Soon we'd be on the water. The eternal Nile.

An early departure was announced for the five-hundred-mile flight from Cairo to Aswan the next morning. I grew increasingly ill during the night. Long before the sun rose or any alarm went off, I lay in bed with the unsettling sensation that my brain was swimming aimlessly inside my skull.

There was little choice but to make it to the airport, though I was barely able to stand up and certainly could not carry a suitcase loaded with more clothing than I had gotten a chance to wear. I sat on the terminal floor while John advanced through the back-and-forth rows of stanchions and ropes, carrying our baggage gradually toward the ticket counter. Then he came back and carried me.

The Aswan High Dam had been the subject of early academic instruction. When I was in elementary school, an art teacher implored the class to go home and impress upon our parents the urgent need to preserve Egyptian artifacts that would be flooded in the creation of the dam. A reservoir to be expanded into Lake Nasser, projected at three hundred miles long, was about to submerge ancient manmade wonders of the world. The dam's purpose was to regulate seasonal but unpredictable flooding of the narrow strip of fertile land along the Nile River that was critically important for agriculture. Rice and sugar cane. Wheat and cotton.

Whether the teacher mentioned alleviating hunger and improving the economy or the displacement of tens of thousands of Nubian people, I do not recall. The archaeological rescue operation was a monumental (pun intended) undertaking in which UNESCO moved twenty architectural entities including Abu Simbel and the temple of Ramses II.

Following a short flight, we transferred to a small wooden boat. It was weathered and squeaky, and it held only a few dozen passengers. This was no deluxe cruise ship for the self-indulgent; we had accepted that.

The excursion agenda took participants into Aswan to sail on a *felucca* to the red-granite site of Elephantine Island and the mausoleum of the late spiritual and political leader Aga Khan III, nearly our contemporary. Feeling queasy, I stayed behind, sitting in a deck chair outside our compartment, trying to maintain a calm head and stomach. I ate very carefully on board that evening in a mess hall with large windows and scant adornment. Soup, not salad. Nothing that wasn't hot. Bottled beverages only. No dessert, a major sacrifice for me at that point in my life. That was the only meal I would ever have onboard.

Our humble craft floated northward toward Luxor, carrying us between two thin ribbons of green only a few yards wide along both sides of the river. There's a miles-long strip of largely manmade oasis supported by irrigating from river water. Not very clean water, I began to suspect. Everything was covered with dust. Even the palm trees looked dirty. Months of dry winds, and no rainfall to wash them clean. Immediately beyond the verdant strip, an abrupt transition to sand. Beige rocks and earth as far as the eye could see in any direction.

The next day the expedition was scheduled to take in the double temple of Kom Ombo and the extraordinarily well preserved Edfu. I'd grown sicker overnight; John should go without me, we decided. He saw the combination of high-relief and low-relief murals in temples. With sunken relief, I suppose an artist might just carve deeper if he's not satisfied with something he's done. In high-relief work, the foreground design stands out from the wall, all the surrounding rock having been carved away. No do-overs here. What's gone is gone.

John and the other travelers saw the Collossi, twin giants at Memnon. I lay on a cot, ailing too badly to turn my head.

After dinner, John returned to our quarters early, and we listened to *muezzin* calls to prayer. *We are definitely not in Kansas, Toto.* The crier's chant was magnified by outdoor loudspeakers mounted on tall mosque minarets. Its intonation was eerie, floating over the lonely, still water. Five daily reminders to pay one's respects to Allah contrasted sharply with some of the guests' behavior. German tourists in the group who wanted to see more of the wide-open spaces gathered on the upper deck to sunbathe. Because they lived in a country whose skies were permanently gray, they were inveterate sun worshippers. When they got the chance, they exposed as much skin as possible to nature's tanning bed. This was not the Heidelberg Neckarwiese but there they were, making themselves at home, topless atop the boat.

When the little craft passed through the locks at Esna to accomplish a twenty-six-foot elevation change, the women's partial nudity gave a total shock to the thobe-clad Muslim men on the docks. They were fifty yards away, but they could see well enough. And we on board could see the whites of their bulging eyes.

With each passing morning and evening on the dingy dinghy, my condition worsened. I barely managed to crawl to the toilet because I passed out any time my head was higher than my heart. My husband would help me in the bathroom, but every time he let go of me, my noggin conked against the wall. Or so I'm told. *For richer, for poorer, in sickness and in health.*

I lay in bed all day on that creaky wooden vessel, nibbling on saltine crackers and trying to drink hot lemon water delivered regularly to my quarters by a kind young waiter. It provided no relief. My heart began racing. A physician in Germany later explained that dehydration puts stress on the vena cava: the heart has to work harder to pump blood through a body with less fluid to circulate. That could drain the color from one's countenance, I suppose.

John felt slightly ill in the night but was sufficiently well to get up in the morning. That day as well, he would tour while I stayed on board with lemon-tea guy.

After a couple of days of vertigo, the crew summoned medical care from town. Maybe someone could give me an antibiotic. Perhaps a penicillin injection. However, when the doctor opened his briefcase, I noticed loose sand in its corners and an unwrapped syringe. "Please," I pleaded in a hoarse whisper. "Don't let him give me a shot. I'll die from something worse than this." Probably a mistake on my part.

The doctor left me with a jar of enormous capsules. Me, a person who hates swallowing pills so badly that her morning vitamins are chewable Flintstones. Big tablets are a nightmare as they scrape against your throat on the way down. Capsules are miserable because they float on that sip of water toward the roof of your mouth, as if afraid of drowning. Can I cut one in half and take the dose in two parts? Nope. That was worse: the contents so bitter I gagged on it immediately.

It turned out that every passenger on that trip got sick, some more than others. I most of all. The only traveler to escape unscathed was the teenager who had discovered the cockroach. Her family said she'd recently had a shot of penicillin for some unrelated reason, and that had bolstered her constitution. Even she got queasy once, but that was likely because of everyone around her being in such a disgusting state.

I had barely consumed anything. How did I get so sick? How was it that we all succumbed to food poisoning? Maybe it wasn't the food. Maybe it was the dishes. I began to envision the kitchen crew piling all the dinner dishes together and rinsing them by dredging them in a big fishing net over the side of the boat. Maybe it was the air. Were there pathogens in the air? Were there malicious spores floating about such that just breathing was enough to infect you?

The Department of Defense teachers offered to pick out souvenirs for me, and John handed them a wad of Egyptian pounds. I wondered: Was it a little intoxicating to indulge a shopping urge while spending someone else's money? Or was it a nerve-racking responsibility? The women returned with packages I never opened until we got home. Things for me to keep and some to give to friends. These are called souvenirs, from the French word for remembrance. Ironic acquisitions for someone with so few memories of a fantastical place. There was a carved-stone mummy in his case. Papyrus weavings suitable for framing. A black scarab-beetle paperweight. Scarves. Strings of beads. A T-shirt with a gold sphinx printed on the front was made of fine-quality (Egyptian?) cotton. I still have that, though the "gold" has long since faded.

On my very last day in the country, I dared trust my body to go with the group to Karnak Temple Complex. We walked through part of the Great Hypostyle Hall, photographed the avenue of criosphinxes with rams' heads. Too weak to complete the trek, I sat on a rock to wait for everyone else. The fresh air and sunshine were soothing. Friendly schoolgirls, in clusters of two or three, approached and asked if they might take pictures with me. "Auntie? Auntie?" Sometimes they wanted my name, occasionally my address. That was all right; none of them ever showed up at my front door.

Back at the Frankfurt airport, I fell into the arms of the friend who came to pick us up. "I got sick," I whimpered. Her expression said, I told you so. If I'd felt better sooner, I might have sought compensation from the travel company, but I didn't have the energy to pursue it.

After I was home for a week or two, I began feeling excessively bloated and miserable. Thanks to German plumbing with a sort of shelf in the toilet bowl, it's easy to collect samples and identify parasites. 'Nuff said.

A visit unfinished in many ways beckons me to return to the land of pharaohs and sphinxes. How I'd love to try again, but I don't dare. There are too many other tropical destinations in which I have yet to contract repugnant conditions. Still, the haunting muezzin sound and the beautiful brown faces of the children are enduringly positive souvenirs.

⁓I⁓

MOROCCO

OUARZAZATE: 'PLACE WITHOUT NOISE'

My travel preparations are logistical. My spouse's are intellectual. He can read so much about a country and its offerings and options that he almost doesn't want to go anymore. It's too hard to set priorities, and we never have time to do everything in the guidebooks. Should we go to northern or southern Morocco? John was so intrigued by both of them, he couldn't decide. A paradox of choice. Maybe we should stay home and watch *The Man Who Knew Too Much*. We had ten days in which to visit this land featuring an ideal combination: The African continent sounded exotic, while the French spoken there would increase my comfort level. We scheduled a resort stay in Ouarzazate at the foot of the Anti-Atlas mountain range, preceded by a few days in Rabat. We had acquaintances there.

***

Taking off from the airport in Germany was the usual breeze of efficiency. Landing in Morocco proved problematic. As we were nearing our destination, the pilot announced that we could not land in Casablanca. We would circle for a while.

My least favorite flight pattern, because a tightly banked arc is sharply angled and bumpy. A short time later, we were informed that we would be rerouted because of troubles with another aircraft immobilized on the Casa tarmac. It could not be moved or unloaded. The airport would be closed for several hours.

Hostage situation? My mind immediately goes to dark places when things don't go as planned in foreign lands.

Eventually our plane left its holding pattern, and we flew to Marrakech instead of Casablanca. The airport was all I saw of the imperial city on that trip, as we waited for another flight. Reality was nothing as extreme as my imagination. A small plane had gotten whipped about by a sand storm and scooted off the runway. After an hour, we were loaded haphazardly onto a different airplane to fly back to Casablanca. This time my seatmate was not my spouse. Details of how this occurred were unclear, but the new plane had a different configuration, and everyone got shuffled at the last minute. Seat assignments were moot. John and I got separated in the rush. *Just sit anywhere.*

Sometimes when you get on a flight, you fall into a pleasant exchange with your seatmate. Sometimes you become new best friends. Sometimes you don't talk at all, intentionally avoid interacting. I ended up next to an attractive young man with dark hair and a trim beard. Karim spoke French, and he began to explain that he was a university student in Frankfurt and was on his way home for the *Fête du Mouton*. Sacrificing of lambs. To gather with family and observe Aïd el-Kebir. We were going to visit friends in Rabat before a week at Club Méditerranée in Ouarzazate, I explained.

We arrived in the dark at a tiny airport with no staff and no town in sight. We had missed our train to Rabat. The only transportation available that day. What to do?

Thank goodness I hadn't gone into hermit mode on the plane. My new friend's father and brothers had come to meet him at the airport. They were to drive him home to where his mother had been preparing his favorite treats and traditional meals of the season. He was confident his father would offer us a ride into town. If we didn't mind squeezing into their little white pickup truck, they could toss our suitcases in the back and give us a ride to the city limits, where we could call our hosts.

John sat up front next to Karim. Being the smallest passenger, I was situated in the backseat, squished between the two brothers. *Do I make conversation or stare quietly ahead and down, focusing my gaze somewhere near my knees?* We were seated so close to each other, I didn't dare turn my face toward either one.

It's harrowing to travel in little foreign cars on narrow, remote roads where the curves are ample and the speed limits unposted. The wind that had caused plane-landing challenges was buffeting the lightweight truck. Even before it began to rain. And then sleet. And then hail. Full-on hailstones battered the truck, pounding on the metal roof and shattering our eardrums. No need to try conversing now. No one could hear anything during that half hour.

Passing us on the tight, twisting highway were many other small trucks. Some of them had beds filled with sheep. It's unclear how the poor lambs tolerated the hailstorm. If they knew what their fate would be a few days hence, they would not have complained about a little solid precipitation anyway.

Our hostess in Rabat, the sister of a grad-school friend, was a lovely and gracious woman who made plans to show us around the city for a couple of days. Laila had arranged a dinner party for us, inviting two other couples. She greeted and welcomed us warmly, though we were late. They were sitting in a candlelit living room because the same storm we had experienced had shut down their electricity. Dinner and diners had been waiting for us for hours.

Her husband was congenial to us but not a friendly person. While our new travel acquaintances had gone out of their way to rescue us, driven us from Casablanca to Rabat, and called our host, Kaysan had declined to come and get us at the proposed rendez-vous point. His car was a Mercedes, he informed these kindly strangers, and he was not about to subject it to a blizzard of hail. The Moroccans in the little pickup drove us all the way across the city to the townhouse. We'd had no idea this uncomfortable negotiating was going on. I noticed the next morning that Kaysan also spoke harshly to the hired help in the kitchen. Which always tells you something about the character of a man.

Laila saw to it that we should visit highlights of Rabat. Grand Mosque. Royal Palace. Kasbah of the Oudayas. The Hassan Tower is appealing for what it is, 144 feet of carved red sandstone, the base of an incomplete minaret, and for what it never became, surrounded as it is with 348 partial stone columns intended to support a major mosque initiative 800 years ago.

We went for a stroll on a beach; this was a side of the Atlantic Ocean I had never seen. Outside the lush Andalusian Gardens, water from brass cups carried on a tray was offered by a *garrab* dressed in the traditional red *djellaba* of his trade and a wide hat ornately trimmed with colorful tassels. He should have been rewarded for his efforts, but I was afraid to drink the water.

On our last day, Laila dropped us at the Rabat railway station, and for an hour we gazed out the train window as the city faded into desert. We passed a village of dingy huts that didn't look like they'd have electricity let alone a refrigerator, but most of them sprouted old TV antennas. What were they watching on television, as tourists flashed past on their way to a Club Med vacation?

***

Ouarzazate is a Berber word meaning "without noise." The town lies near the junction of the rugged Dadès Gorges and the Drâa Valley. It gives access to the Road of a Thousand Kasbahs, a scenic route dotted with Berber villages. This was the site of a rustic and short-lived Club Med resort. From here we visited the Kasbah town of Aït Benhaddou and the Old Synagogue, and made minor outings to a grocery store and Internet café with waiting lines, old computers, and iffy connections.

On a Club-sponsored bus trip through the desert, a comfort break offered a small brick building with a narrow door and no windows. It was pitch black inside. Not a ray of light. We'd been informed there were no porcelain fixtures. Was there a pit? A trench? I had no idea. I backed out of that room and decided I'd rather traipse over to the other side of a sand dune to find a little privacy.

Shopping at a souk that afternoon I was, as always, consumed by the scents of spices and the sights of bright clothing and pottery typical of an open-air market. Beyond the souk was a warren of private residences. A boy of about eight, wearing a plain cloth robe, wanted to be given a few coins for leading us through an adobe maze to his family's quarters. My eyes were riveted to the sight of a skinned lamb hanging in their open doorway. A girl of about twelve rebuked her little brother and exercised her right to forbid photography.

Back at the lodge on the desert, meals were exotic and varied. Cooked vegetable dishes were plentiful, sumptuous, and safe. Since my stomach gets upset in tropical climates, I declined salads and fresh fruits. This behavior prompted the French guests at our table to offer their critique. "Oh, you just get sick because you're an American," they said. John defended me against this accusation. In his own way.

"She's not purely American. Half of her is French," he retorted. "The annoying half."

The chef offered a guided tour of which tagines contained quasi-medicinal herbs that would prevent gastroenteritis. That right there should tell you something.

Lounging around the hotel property and overindulging in rich buffet meals seemed too sedentary, so we opted for an overnight camping trip to the dunes. This would involve riding for several hours in a Jeep across the Drâa Valley, a wide expanse of dirt that used to be covered in much-needed river water.

We were a dozen tourists from various nations with a local guide as our driver. The weather was breezy at first, not unwelcome under a cloudless sky. Then the wind began to pick up velocity. Sand started blowing through the vehicle. Our clothes. Our hair. Dunes were shifting in real time. How could the driver have any idea where we were supposed to be going?

Then suddenly we were going nowhere. The Jeep got stuck in loose sand more than once, and everyone had to get out to push it until the tires cleared the ruts.

Still the sand pelted us and obscured our view. Of what? There was no road. The sun was lost in the gray-brown haze. Passengers were starting to get nervous. Was this a regular part of the agenda?

"Oh, it's probably like this a lot," John said. "Our driver has probably seen much worse. Ask him, so everybody can calm down."

Translating into French, I passed along my husband's inquiry. "We're looking for reassurance that you're used to these conditions."

"Oh, no!" the driver replied. "I've lived here since I was born, and this is the worst storm I've ever seen in my life."

Thanks, John. Great idea.

***

It was late afternoon when we got to a campsite that Club Med workers had set up for us a day earlier. Tents and dishes and dinner and a water tank. Stereo amplifiers and a carpet for a performers' stage.

Long before we arrived at the site, all the dining and bunk tents had been flattened by the hard-flung sand. The combined efforts of staff and tourists were insufficient to shovel the heavy piles of dirt off the canvas or re-right the tent poles. That would have to wait. Our hosts had sent word (heaven only knows how) to the resort management requesting all new everything. Except for belly dancers. They were the true-grit originals.

The winds gradually subsided, and while we waited for replacement equipment and supplies, we were able to walk through the Anti-Atlas dunes, observing wave after wave in this otherworldly scape. The adventure we'd come here for. The trick is to wander out far enough that you feel a deliciously untethered solitude. Then turn back toward camp before you get hopelessly lost.

We watched the dust settle out of the sky like a window shade being lowered ever so slowly. Above the fuzzy line halfway up the horizon, blue sky. Below that interface, beigeness all the way down.

When we returned from dune trekking, clean tableware had been set up. Too soon, because the dust was settling so slowly that everything was once again covered with silt by the time we sat down to dinner. Lift a plate or plastic drinking glass, and a bare, clean circle emerged on the tablecloth.

Following the meal, a fresh, patterned wool carpet was rolled over a flat place on the ground. Sitting in our dusty hiking clothes, we watched voluptuous belly dancers perform to Arabic music in their flashy red-and-gold costumes.

After dark, the sky was beautifully clear, filled with moonlight and an impossible number of stars. The sand storm had cleaned the air as effectively as a monsoon rain wipes smog out of a cityscape. We finally began to relax. One traveler, a Swiss cellist, asked our driver to sing her a lullaby. "*Nini ya moumou.*" She leaned her head close in to his. Then she lay her head on his shoulder. Then I decided it was time for me to go to bed.

There wasn't enough water for everyone to use the improvised shower, and we would have turned into mudballs anyway. I rinsed my face, called it good, and slept in my clothes as the desert temperature dropped precipitously.

Lying on narrow cots, it was hard to get to sleep. Indistinct voices from another tent murmured while we pondered the events of the day. I lay silent, getting up only once to go to the makeshift bathroom. In the morning a Frenchman accused John and me of having talked all night, keeping him awake.

When we returned to the resort the next afternoon, we were instantly recognizable to those who had not gone on the excursion. "You! You were on that trip, weren't you?" they'd gasp. Our caked skin and hair were dead giveaways. We would be rinsing dirt from our scalps, ears, and noses for days to come. But we enjoyed hero status for the rest of the week.

UNITED ARAB EMIRATES

It was not so long ago that half a million people living on a small portion of the Arabian Peninsula south of the Strait of Hormuz inhabited tents or houses built with bricks mixed from mud, clay, stone, and maybe coral. Nomadic Bedouin tribes constructed tents out of thick fabric woven from the hair of goats and camels. They survived by herding and hunting and through fishing, pearl diving, and date cultivation. It was 1939 when an Indian physician arrived in Dubai to establish the first modern health clinic. Seven emirates formed the United Arab Emirates in 1971-72 under the leadership of Sheikh Zayed bin Sultan Al Nahyan. Today, Dubai is internationally famous for futuristic and sometimes whimsical architecture, including Burj Khalifa, the tallest building in the world, and Palm Jumeirah, an exclusive artificial archipelago shaped like a palm tree three miles in diameter. Memories of the UAE that I share here reflect observations made just a few short years ago. However, the culture, like the skyline, is changing every day.

FIVE STAR, THIRD WORLD

House-hunting was not an issue in the Emirates, as it had been in Germany. The university that was hiring John provided lodging for its professors. Faculty members with children went into compounds in various neighborhoods. Many of the others were assigned to housing in an apartment building.

Our place was clean, bright, and light. White inside and out. White ceramic-tile floors. A wall of windows and a small, narrow balcony with glass parapets where you might grow plants and do a weather check in the morning. Not that the weather was especially changeable.

The building was brand new. This pleased me because my compulsive cleaning only required wiping up the chalk dust of sheetrock and paint, and not some strangers' detritus.

The 25-story structure was newer than new: it was not quite finished. Little repairs were ongoing. Deliver a refrigerator. Connect the thermostat. Test the intercom. Spackle and paint the settling cracks that zigzagged the block walls. They had to be patched this month so they could crack again in the same places next month.

Our flat had two bedrooms and two bathrooms, one of them with a bidet, the other with a leaky ceiling. Over the shower, plaster became sodden and started peeling.

One morning while showering before work, my dear husband called out to me: "Hey, Baby, would you come in here please? And bring a spatula."

Whoa! This is a come-on line I've never heard before.

As he was showering, patches of plaster were falling on his head. He wanted a metal pancake-turner so he could reach up and proactively peel off the rest of the hanging shards.

I began to refer to the piping, rather uncharitably, as "plumbing brought to you by people who have never used any."

Large blue buckets were stationed in the apartment corridors to catch water leaking through the ceiling panels. Small men in navy-blue uniforms would empty them periodically. Sometimes they sat in the hallways for hours so they could swap out containers before they overflowed.

There were a lot of jobs like that in the Emirates. Once while we were driving in Dubai, we passed a big cube of a building in the early stages of construction. Its frame was steel girders and concrete, but there were no walls. Sitting in the middle of it, on the fifth or sixth floor, was a small, dark man in a navy-blue uniform. There didn't seem to be anything to steal, but there he was, guarding it.

The ceiling leaks were so pervasive, on every level of the building, that I sometimes had visions of the entire high-rise dissolving in a mound of wet chalk. Like a giant white cow pie.

The kitchen had ample cabinets in a pale natural-wood finish, and self-closing drawers. If you gave a drawer the gentlest push, a hidden spring would automatically pull it completely and quietly shut.

All the appliances were brushed stainless steel. A full-sized refrigerator. With the door opening the wrong way. Right beside that, a little washing machine. It was an efficient front-loading model with a window. This feature was helpful in identifying things clanking in an unexpectedly noisy load. Usually, the offending item was a cellphone or a blood-glucose monitor glowing eerily in the dark sudsy water. You couldn't retrieve it until the load had completed its run. A stainless-steel range and oven, which we never used. Not because we were loath to cook or to clean it. Because the natural gas was not connected during the four years we lived there.

The first holiday season, the management delivered a full, hot, multi-course dinner for each family. It was much like an American Thanksgiving meal.

At the front corner of the lot, near an intersection, was a massive utility box labeled "natural gas." For a long time, we thought there must be logistical or technical delays in getting it hooked up. A year later, we learned that contract disagreements were preventing installation. After a few more months, residents were asked if they wanted to pay to have gas available for cooking in their units. For a hookup fee. We decided the microwave oven was adequate. Just think how much I saved on Easy-Off oven cleaner.

Air conditioning was sufficient for the job of cooling 400 units where the outdoor temperatures might be 111 Fahrenheit in the afternoon and 88 at night. The electricity was more or less reliable. This would seem to be a good thing, except for that questionable combination: hot wires running through wet walls?

Although the bedrooms had built-in closets with sliding doors, we needed additional shelving and a dining set to double as a desk. These we procured, along with our cohort of new professors, on a bus trip to an Ikea-like store.

Our home was an ample 1,600 square feet, much of that space intended for a living/dining great room. It always echoed since we had so little furniture and no carpets.

On my neighborhood walks, I spied a few discarded items set on a sidewalk curb. One piece was a black Sony TV stand. For several days, I pondered it.

"John," I said, "I'm sure that's free for the taking. Let's get it."

He balked. So I went into the apartment complex and asked a security guard if I could have it. He said no. Then I talked to the secretary, and she didn't mind at all: "Who'd want that old thing?"

I would.

It was heavy, awkward, and bulky; it barely fit into the little Toyota. In the lobby of our building, we asked an employee to help us get it from the car into the elevator, then into our apartment. It had spent several days in Abu Dhabi dust, so I slid it into the back bathroom and hosed it off with the spigot from the bidet.

We never had a TV to set on it, but it was useful for books.

Now we needed some seating. By and by we answered an ad for a used L-shaped sectional. We called the seller, who said it was still available and promised it was in good condition. Yes, we could come and look at it after work. Just before I hung up, he warned me that he would not dicker on the price.

When we got to the man's place, we learned that he was an Abu Dhabi policeman. Two other young men were there watching television. While the Abu cop talked with us, it was hard not to notice that his guests were watching a recording of *Mission Impossible: Ghost Protocol*.

The sofa was acceptable: black leather with coarse white top-stitching. We had no way of transporting it, but the seller said he had a friend who could deliver it. He placed a call, and much Arabic dialogue ensued. The friend was not available, but he recommended someone else. It was pretty easy to find a couple of strong young guys to hire short-term. They would come right away.

The movers rang the bell downstairs, and our salesman/host buzzed them in. He opened his apartment door and glanced down the long corridor to watch them approach.

"Oh my God!" He closed the door. "You are going to be afraid. Oh, I don't know if you will go with them. You will probably think they are terrorists."

He reopened the door, and in came two scruffy-looking men with long hair, drab-colored robes, and leather sandals. Judging by their garb, they were likely from Pakistan near the Afghan border. One man wore a brown salwar kameez. His glossy hair was dark and curly, and he sported a mustache. The other man was in a beige cotton tunic and pants with a coarsely woven belt at his waist. His black hair was unruly; his beard was so thick you could barely see his mouth. They spoke no English but seemed harmless enough.

John paid them, and they hoisted the sofa down the stairs and out to the sidewalk below. It was past sunset by now. The seller watched the movers load and tie down our new used furniture into a little turquoise pickup truck with steel railing around its bed.

Now... how to explain where we lived? Our not-terrorist hires would have to follow John's car and try not to get lost in the traffic in the dark.

But wait! My life partner had a better idea: I should jump into the front of the pickup truck with these two guys and show them the way in case they lost sight of his car.

Right. Because I'm such a great navigator. And I'm not afraid of strange men in an unfamiliar city. At night.

The men followed us home successfully and carried the sofa set up to our apartment. They already knew they were somewhat of a curiosity to us, so John was bold enough to ask if we could take their picture. The back page of our next Christmas letter featured a photo of a sturdy white professor engaging the Middle Eastern gig economy.

***

On the ground floor of our complex were gyms with exercise equipment and lockers. Men and women had separate workout rooms. Outside were a shared swimming pool and, perhaps extraneous given the climate, a hot tub.

Below that was a multi-level parking garage with assigned spaces for every resident. One vehicle per apartment, which was adequate. Our new car was a Toyota Yaris subcompact. The model name amused me, because when we'd moved to Germany for a second stint, our best friends found us a lightly used car whose name sounded like Yaris. It was a Mitsubishi Galant, but Reinhardt referred to it as a *jahreswagen*. A one-year car. German rental car companies updated their fleets annually, selling the previous year's purchases at a discount. Decades later, here we were again in a Yaris-wagon.

IN-PROCESSING

You didn't just buy a plane ticket to Abu Dhabi and start job hunting. You had to be highly motivated to go there, or the bureaucratic requirements would overwhelm you.

You applied for a job, submitted references, got interviewed, secured a job offer, and negotiated your contract. You went for inoculations and renewed your passport so it would be valid for your expected length of stay plus six months.

That was the easy part.

We had to find nearly every official document that testified to our existence and status in the world. We couldn't make Xerox copies of anything. We had to acquire new originals from all over the country.

Birth certificates were required. If you were a military kid born on an overseas base that no longer existed, you had to secure a consular report to prove you had been an American citizen from birth and brought legally into the USA.

Proof that we were legally wed. No cohabitation allowed, so we got a notarized marriage license from the

State of Arizona and provided it to United Arab Emirates Embassy in Washington, DC.

Education credentials. It didn't matter if you had a Ph.D.; the hiring organization wanted to see all the academic certifications you'd earned before that one, all the way back to high school. So we tracked down public-school documents in Arizona. We contacted a county clerk's office in New York to get notarized versions of university diplomas. Course transcripts were considered superior to diplomas, even though one might think that these could be more easily forged. So we obtained notarized copies of those too from our universities in New York and Massachusetts and Maryland, got them approved by the relevant counties, and then sent them to the State Department for authentication.

Pay minor fees at each stage.

We now had a stack of impressive papers. Or at least, an impressive stack of papers. These were supposed to be verified through a cumbersome chain of attestation steps akin to the *apostille* system of The Hague. Electronic files were not accepted at any stage.

The information had to get to the US Department of State.

And back to us.

Then to the Embassy.

On time.

An ambitious, conscientious person might ascertain all required steps in the process, then begin to undertake said steps. The aforementioned person will shortly decide to hire one of the professionals who has a magical way of making each procedure happen in the prescribed order and with necessary efficiency. They did not seem to be verifying any of the contents. They simply proved that someone had submitted these pieces of paper to some mediating party. I imagined a young man riding a bicycle around the capital city with our dossiers.

Pay considerable fees at this stage. In exchange, receive many official- (or officious-) looking documents with gold-foil seals, illegible signatures, and red-ink rubber stamps.

Lastly, John had to compose a letter stating that he did not object to his wife's working should she choose to seek employment.

No charge for that.

***

Every foreign individual arriving in the United Arab Emirates underwent extensive review of a medical-history questionnaire. Then a lung X-ray. For this procedure, a woman went into a changing cabin with a curtain. She was given not a gown, not a thin paper drape, but a full-length yellow wraparound made of heavy cloth-like paper with elasticized fabric ribbing at the cuffs of the long sleeves.

The radiologic imaging took a few seconds. Then the gown was thrown into the trash bin. This happened a hundred times a day.

~I~

DIABETIC IN DUBAI

Every three days an insulin-dependent person has to change the infusion set or pod on her pump. In addition to carting around equipment, supplies, cold-packed insulin and extra backups, she must schedule the semiweekly replacements around travel or other activities. For me, this routine went fine the first time I did it at our hotel in the United Arab Emirates.

Great. I can do this.

Three days later it didn't go so well. We were on our way to meet new colleagues for dinner, and it seemed advisable to change my pump first. This time, when I inserted a cannula under my skin, it stabbed a blood vessel and, as my father might have told childhood me, I sprang a leak. A Kleenex was not enough to catch the flow. *Where's a styptic pen when you need one?* I reached for a washcloth and lay down flat on the cool tile floor. The terrycloth soaked through. I folded it in four and applied pressure. That didn't stanch the flow either. The spread of red was stunning.

Hmmm. I'm not afraid. More inconvenienced. Why does this have to happen when we're in a hurry?

Still, the thought occurs: What if the bleeding doesn't stop? What if I were to injure myself in some other way? Do we know where a hospital is? Is there a local equivalent of a 911 phone call? I have no idea.

Note to self: Check into that tomorrow.

***

Some weeks later I had an excellent consultation with medical staff at Imperial College London Diabetes Centre. It was within walking distance of our new apartment. Fees were reasonable, and our university offered health insurance.

As with most expatriates, my medical care was provided by foreign practitioners and institutions. Cleveland Clinic. American Hospital. The doctors were from England, India, the USA. Many were Arabic; scarcely any were Emirati.

What I didn't know was that there were many Emirate physicians. They practiced in Emirati hospitals clinics that may not look modern or flashy, but whose staff included teams of experts in cardiology, oncology, ophthalmology, trauma. The patients were mostly Emirati. They were getting the best medical care oil money could buy. Foreigners living in the bubble of expat housing compounds moved about largely unaware of them.

LIQUOR LICENSE

Passport. Military ID card. US Army Europe driver permit. Library card. Red Cross VolunTeen ID. It's fun to glance at old identity cards stuffed in the back of the SentrySafe firebox. One of my favorites is a United Arab Emirates liquor license.

This is not a permit to sell liquor. It's permission to buy liquor in the Islamic country or to consume it in one of the few authorized locations such as private, international-chain hotels.

As at a Class VI shop on a military installation, we had to show this ID when we went into the restricted outlets that sold packaged beer, wine, and hard liquor. In the UAE, shoppers would exit the store carrying large, dark brown, opaque plastic bags that were telltale for their lack of brand labeling. Almost every customer was a foreigner. Occasionally we would see Emirati men making purchases. I pretended not to notice them. Which sorts of status or special dispensation they may have had I do not know. Nor where they went to consume it, as it was not legal to serve alcohol to Muslim Emiratis even at home.

"How do you know they were Emirati?" a friend in America asked me.

"By the way they dress. In the white *kandura*."

"Couldn't anyone dress like that?"

I suppose they could, but no one would dare to.

The Emirati man's robe is full length and fashioned from high-quality white fabric. It fits him well, regardless of his size. The design features a high banded neckline, covered buttons, reinforced cuffs, and a silk-threaded *sharaba* tassel. If you look at a man closely (which of course I would never do!) you can detect a long undershirt beneath.

Anyone might wear a kandura. It's modest, cool, and comfortable. It can be seen in a range of colors: beige, pale blue, sage green. The material is usually a dull, thin cotton. Men of all sorts of occupations and nationalities wear them in the Emirates. But not just anyone wears the tailored white Emirati kandura with the handmade tassel.

ASPECTS OF ABAYAS

A little Emirati girl can be as frilly and free as any western child. Her lacy pink dress, bare legs and dark, loose-flowing hair remind me of the girls I used to see in their Easter Sunday finery in Nogales.

Then one day she dons *abaya* and *shayla*, and you barely recognize her.

She's a big girl now, entering adolescence and approaching womanhood.

The abaya is a long black robe covering a woman from neck to wrist and ankle. It limits a woman's capacity to make much of a fashion statement. And it's got to be hot in the sunshine.

The shayla is a long, black headscarf. It covers thick, shiny tresses. A woman's crowning glory, the Bible says. In conservative circles, only immediate family will ever get to admire that beautiful hair.

In one of the sunniest climes in the world, women are cloaked head to toe in steamy ebony. Black robes modest and opaque. They don't show dirt easily, but they need to retain their color through many washings. Big bottles of liquid laundry detergent caught my attention at Lulu Hypermarket because they were made of black plastic. Persil, a brand I recognized from living in Germany, offered a version labeled Abaya Shampoo. The liquid itself was dark bluish gray, formulated to keep dark colors dark.

There was also a white kandura wash for men's clothes, and I often wondered how much labor it must take to keep the men's full-length robes impeccably brilliant. I did not much wonder who was performing that labor.

While the Emirati men all dressed alike, the women found ways to escape homogeneity. Some were adorned with contrasting metallic embroidery or crystal rhinestones from Austria.

Despite what the drab covering might suggest, clothing underneath the conservative abaya may be much more colorful. Flamboyant even. Stunning examples were revealed to me at women-only parties and wedding receptions.

At the university where my husband taught in the Emirates, the school uniform was essentially the ubiquitous costume of Emirati women. It protected their modesty and could be seen as a great leveler of social status. As to the latter function, it was not entirely successful. Shoe styles by Gucci and Lanvin peeked out beneath flowing gowns as women walked. Many students carried designer handbags. Chanel. Dior. Hermès. Prada. One English teacher commented that if just a few of them would leave their purses behind when they exited the classroom, she could sell them and retire.

Not every student appeared to be wealthy. While most of their abayas were well made from quality fabric, a few students wore imitations. Coarser material, not quite black, with inelegant zippers. Those students were probably Arabic but not Emirati.

Students on the women's side of the campus were subjected to public announcements about keeping their abayas fastened securely from top to bottom. No brightly hued skirt should peek out at the hem or show through a front slit when she walked too fast.

John was bold enough to inquire how his students felt about these reminders.

"We agree that we should dress modestly" was the consensus. "But we don't like to be told to do it."

So, all the female students wore black. All had dark skin and eyes and covered-up hair. Yet Dr. John was impressively adept at recognizing faces and learning names. He did not find that "they all look alike." Occasionally, he could be fooled, however. A student would show up one day wearing a *niqab*, a scarf covering the lower part of her face. She'd be sitting in her usual place, but he would have trouble figuring out who she was. She would have to remind him of her name.

"You don't usually cover your face," he once protested in defense of his confusion.

"I got married," the young woman replied. "My parents didn't care, but my new in-laws insist on it."

The school dress code was not necessarily burdensome, according to a student who befriended me and took me shopping for gifts for my family. Sometimes it's a relief to cover yourself when you leave the house, she told me. You could go to school wearing your pajamas, and who would know? There's no such thing as a bad hair day.

That almost sounds liberating.

The population at our apartment was more mixed than that at school. It exemplified a range of customs. The gym on the second floor had separate workout rooms for men and women, but the rooftop swimming pool was shared. Some Muslim women using the common outdoor pool wore *burkinis*. These are colorful, loose-fitting wetsuits that cover the figure from head to toe. They allow modesty and freedom of movement, but they take on a lot of water that has to be dragged out of the pool and extensively drip dried. A woman in a blue, black, and white tankini enjoyed some respite from the heat, though I imagine the synthetic material would be oppressive if she didn't get into the water right away. Her face was not covered, but with the built-in hood that fit like a skull cap, she looked like a penguin.

A friend from Casablanca told me she might appreciate the option of using gender-segregated beaches, where women could feel free and unobserved in form-fitting activewear. However, these locations were not available in Morocco at that time because of concerns that religious fundamentalists could weaponize such an opportunity, forcing all women onto female-only beaches or banning them from the beach entirely. And what would come next? Forbidding them to enjoy public parks? The risk of inhibiting women's freedom was too great.

EQUAL BUT SEPARATE

The historically all-female university where John taught expanded to a co-ed facility and moved to a new campus before we arrived. Like a butterfly, the building was designed as two large wings, each with dozens of classrooms and offices. A female side and a male side.

The campus was situated on a large piece of desert property, but the external grounds were rarely used. Everything, including all of the parking, was covered for protection from the sun. Each side of the facility featured a long mall. There faculty, staff, and students could gather, enjoy a coffee, or do a bit of shopping at one of a few small stores: a stationery boutique, health-food store, flower shop. The mall ceiling was three commercial stories high. To view the women's side from a second- or third-floor landing at lunchtime was to be transported to Hogwarts Great Hall, overlooking hundreds of young people in long black robes.

Exhibitions were held there too. These might be art shows or displays of academic projects and awards. Occasionally, an indigenous replica offered an opportunity to try on traditional costumes including a *burqa,* the metallic partial facemask worn by Bedouin women in past generations. One day a patriotic parade featured children marching in military uniforms and carrying toy rifles. A professor from famously neutral Switzerland was appalled.

The two wings of the campus were connected by a thorax with two dining halls and a library in the middle. As there was only one library, it had to be shared, but never concurrently. Women could use the research and study facility on three days of the week, and men on two days. Even the parking lots were segregated: one for male students, one for female.

On day one of the fall semester, a first-year professor from England, new to the country, greeted his students on the men's campus. After handing out the syllabus to a roomful of white-kandura-clad students, he noted that they needed textbooks. The stack was too heavy to carry, so he had not brought them with him.

"We could help you carry them," one of the young males suggested.

"Yeah?"

"Sure."

"Well... OK."

So off they went, two dozen male students following their teacher out of the classroom, down the hall, through the men's cafeteria, past the uniformed guard, beyond the library, through the women's cafeteria, and into the textbook storeroom. On the women's campus.

The professor handed out the texts, and everyone filed back toward the classroom. It is not known whether any students in white kanduras caught sight of any students in black abayas, but

administrators found out about the little excursion, and the teacher was reprimanded for leading it.

***

Male and female students were forbidden from crossing into one another's campus territory, but faculty members could come and go as they pleased. Men or women could be instructors for either women or men. It was almost as though professors had no gender.

This "otherly" status was not completely blind to gender. Men and women were never to touch. A male professor was careful to never get too close to his students, never lean too close over a computer they were working at, and never touch a book held in a woman's hand. When a female student made an appointment to come to a male professor's office, he would have an extra chair available because she might be more comfortable bringing a friend with her.

The point was repeatedly emphasized in the fall-semester faculty orientation (a weeklong event). Never touch a woman.

"What if she's stumbling? What if she's falling down the stairs?"

"Let her fall. You may not touch her."

A professor from Jordan corroborated the principle. When a female student of his in Amman had an epileptic seizure, her classmates would not allow him to provide first aid. "Don't touch her," they warned. "You'll make trouble for her."

In any foreign country and culture, we try to respect local laws and customs. Their land, their rules. This directive, however, John found intolerable. "If that ever happens, I may get thrown out of the country, but I'm not going to stand by and let someone get hurt," he said. Fortunately, he was never put to that particular test.

***

The curriculum included courses addressing computer ethics and green computing in the desert. Rather than launching into lectures on Immanuel Kant's categorical imperative or John Stuart Mill's utilitarianism, John delved into Islamic ethics. While separate from the Qur'an, Islamic ethics are not secular like some western approaches. They are based on Mohammed's life and decision-making and therefore, more relevant to these students.

As in America, whenever John addressed professional ethics, he reminded learners that a question that seems clear-cut in the classroom may become a more complex dilemma in the real world. For example, it might be corporate management that makes a decision to present false data on a vehicle's fuel efficiency, but if you're an engineer or a computer programmer at the company, you could be the one required to implement the plan. How will you decide? What if a big new data center promises to bring good jobs to your local economy, but it's going to use more water and electricity than your community can afford? What will you do? Or, say you find data mining to be a fascinating field to enter. How do you feel about the way the information might be used?

"You might think there's only one right answer and you know where you stand," he would tell them. "But when the boss is pressuring you, and you have children to feed and bills to pay, alternatives may look more cloudy. If you give some thought now to a few potential scenarios, your decision might be easier down the road."

In a broad-ranging ethics class, Zaynab, one of John's most-accomplished students, told of a relevant personal experience. She was once honored for her charitable service work at a ceremony attended by upper-class officials including members of the royal family. One of the top

Emirati leaders was in the receiving line to congratulate the students. A woman on the stage gave Zaynab a plaque with her name on it while shaking her hand. In the confusion of the moment, Zaynab still had her right arm extended when she approached the next official, the high-ranking sheikh.

The protocol was for the sheikh to politely shake any extended hand. Protocol also allows a woman to cross her right arm over her heart and nod respectfully in lieu of shaking hands with a man. Zaynab had been too flustered to do that in time. Since she didn't withhold her arm, he extended his. Once she saw his hand extended, it seemed too late to cross her chest. She didn't dare rebuff a sheikh, so she felt obliged to shake his hand.

"I felt terrible for a week," she exclaimed, still expressing discomfort years later.

Not every local person took the same stance on the issue. Another female student in the same ethics class related that she had once fainted in a drug store while waiting for a prescription. A man in line behind her saw her wavering and reached out to catch her. After the incident, she apologized to her mother: "I'm sorry. I let a strange man touch me." Her mother reacted without hesitation: "I'm glad he kept you from falling on the floor. You could have hurt yourself otherwise."

These are classic cases of the tension between ethical Islamic practice and tribal customs. Cultural norms may prohibit men from touching female strangers. Islamic maxims call for preserving life, judging acts based on intention, and acknowledging that a greater harm may be eliminated by application of a lesser harm.

***

Before college, John's students had attended traditional, unimaginative public schools that emphasized rote memorization. Some of these young women were quite bright, and a few were ambitious. However, many of them lacked the educational foundation to do college work in fields like math and computer science. Part of the problem was that they'd gone to public schools where foreign teachers presented every subject in English, a language not supported at home. Not an easy way to learn mathematics.

"Lemonade stand" is a class assignment that introduces accounting concepts through a simplified but realistic business scenario. The exercise requires students to figure out the steps required to make and sell lemonade. The curriculum had offered them no accounting background. Still, the students in a computer course on enterprise systems had to figure out the cost of goods, set an appropriate sales price, and produce a balance sheet.

When John introduced the project, twenty-five students looked puzzled.

Make and sell lemonade?

"You know how to use a recipe, right?"

Blank looks. They knew what a recipe was, but they had never used one. Every household had a cook, hired from a foreign country, perhaps the Philippines or Indonesia. They never made lemonade. And selling anything at a makeshift stand in front of their homes would be unimaginable. Still, a cultural gap did not seem to be the problem.

Given a recipe for 50 liters of lemonade, they could not figure out the cost of ingredients required to produce one glassful and how to price it to make a profit.

Homework assignments like this one were sometimes done and sometimes not. When John would remind his students of the deadline for an important "deliverable" component of a semester-long project, they would agree to do it, *Insha'Allah*.

Insha'Allah is a formidable word in the Arabic language and Muslim culture. It means, "If God so wills." The phrase is doubly meaningful to me, and I adopted it readily. First, as a journalist, I was trained not to write, for example, that a school board was going to take a certain action; rather, the board members had announced that they planned to do so. Second, as a God-fearing person, I appreciated the reminder that my best-laid plans may not come to fruition.

When John and I say Insha'Allah, it means, "Good Lord willin' and the crick don't rise." When Emirati students said it, it meant, "That's probably not going to get done on time."

***

While not all of the students were academically brilliant, they were pleasant to teach, because they were polite and respectful in the classroom. They seemed interested in the subject matter and a little curious about their foreign professors as well.

When Dr. John mentioned that his wife would be coming from the United States soon, his female students seemed eager to meet me. I showed up one day when two of my husband's students were passing by his office. They stepped inside, and one of them immediately called a third friend. Her speech was quick and breathless when she exclaimed into her phone, "Come here. Come right now. Mrs. John is here!"

Though they were all eighteen or older, it was hard not to refer to these young women as *girls*. They liked to bring flowers and frequently offered little gifts with childlike enthusiasm. This is why a ceramic plaque in our hallway bears the inscription, "Children are born with wings. Teachers help them to fly." They shared an appealing sense of freshness and energy. Such was their *joie de vivre*.

On a stormy February day, students were so excited they couldn't sit still in a classroom. It was raining. This might only happen twenty days a year in the UAE, so when it does it's an occasion. The young women ran down the halls and burst outdoors, laughing and squealing, and tilting their heads toward the sky to let the pouring rain splash on their hands and faces. Two of them commandeered a three-wheeled mini loader used by the gardeners; one stood on the back while the other steered the wagon through puddles.

There was a certain naïveté which was enviable if slightly concerning. The students expressed great trust in a government that took good care of them. Our young friend Huda expressed little concern when an American woman was stabbed to death in a shopping mall restroom at the high-end Boutik Mall on Reem Island. The news report emphasized the female perpetrator's Yemeni origins, a common scapegoat. There was no public follow-up. We asked Huda what she thought of the ordeal.

"I assume the police took care of the matter," she said simply.

Male college students didn't necessarily have any tighter grip on the realities of the country's transitional status.

"What do you want to do after you graduate?" John typically asked all of his students.

"I want to work in an office," one young man replied, pleased with himself for having a ready response.

"Okay... Doing what?"

"It doesn't matter. Just work in an office."

"Well, if you're going to sit at a desk all day, it might be more pleasant to being doing something you like."

***

Fall-orientation leaders had told new professors they would never get to know students outside the classroom, never meet their parents. *Was that prediction or admonition?*

They were wrong. For most of the professors, it probably was true. Not for us.

People gave us presents. I was invited to a wedding. We were asked to attend camel races, international festivals, student presentations, coffee outings, evening dessert at cafés with students' parents, and dinner in private homes.

We drove all across town to meet the family of one of John's students in her home. Dinner was served on a large blanket-like tablecloth on the living room floor. Some dishes we would eat with our hands. There would be fresh tabbouleh salad. Fragrant *majboos* chicken. Sweet, crispy *luqaimat*. When we were called to gather for dinner, I waited to be shown where I should sit. Not because I expected table and chairs to appear but because I thought we should wait for the young woman in the kitchen to join us. She was the hired help.

Senior student Amna and a friend of hers were permitted to meet John and me for coffee on a Friday afternoon at Mushrif Mall, a multilevel shopping center whose focal point was an aquarium with an elevator rising through the middle of it. Shoppers could glide effortlessly upward while tropical fish floated downward all around them. A father or brother would drive the women to the mall, presumably hover nearby, then pick them up for the ride home. In John's inimitable way, he was able to get insights about this chaperoning and female freedom. I commented that maybe it protected them; there didn't seem to be too many unwed mothers in the Emirates.

"No, I think if such a thing occurred, her father would have the right to have her put to death," Amna said. She glanced at her companion for confirmation. "Yes, I think that's right."

She delivered this information nonchalantly. The way one might address a question about travel plans for next summer. The indication that she was not even sure about the policy conveyed how irrelevant the question was to her life.

***

Why would a U.S. couple be so welcome in an Arabic country? I've always believed it was because my husband was unabashedly American. He never wanted to offend our hosts, but he had insatiable curiosity that demanded quenching. When he drew on his plainspoken Midwest-farm-family background, it was irresistible.

Thus, he could easily ask female students about topics like chaperoning or dress codes and abayas. No one took offense at his questions, and he always got answers.

NOT A DRY HEAT

Mad dogs and Englishmen, my Uncle Homer used to say. That's who goes out in the heat of the day. While my spouse is teaching at a university in the Arabian Desert, I venture out. Carrefour hypermarket is two blocks away, nearly visible from our high-rise. I can make it there on foot to pick up a few groceries. To examine exotic produce and to people-watch.

My eyes are bigger than my knapsack, and I buy too much to carry. It's hotter out than when I left the apartment, probably 120 degrees Fahrenheit. And humid, 75 percent or more. *Where does all this moisture come from in the desert?*

Taxis keep passing and beeping, trying to sell me a ride, but I decline. It's not that far to my building. *I can do this, acclimate.*

A wave of wooziness hits me, and I stop for a few moments. Set the bags down. Sip some water. Take deep breaths. Think cool thoughts. Go home and take a nap.

***

On many evenings, when the temperatures were bearable, John and I walked around our new neighborhood. Past numerous buildings under construction. Past large, round manholes colored according to utility. Red for electrical lines. Blue for potable water. Green for irrigation water. Yellow for fire-hydrants. Grey and square for chilled water. Black square for sewage. Other configurations for fiber optic cable or "earth rod" electrical grounding. Sometimes a baby sand dune, five feet across and rippled with waves, had formed on a sidewalk. I marveled at it the way I'd hover over a horned lizard on a hike in Arizona.

We would stop a couple of minutes to watch the Liwa Building's nightly light show. This was an oddly shaped office building that had a solid base and bulged irregularly in the middle like an asymmetrical vase. In the daytime it was a twenty-story block of Swiss cheese, red Leicester in color, but at night its one thousand windows shone bright green, cobalt blue, purple, and red. Usually the hues appeared sequentially, changing ever minute or so, but occasionally the various colors would form a pattern such as the UAE flag.

After that we might wander through the foreign-embassy district. Diplomatic headquarters of places we had been and places we would never get to see. Afghanistan, Bangladesh, Egypt, India, Iraq, Kuwait, Pakistan, South Korea, Syria, Turkey. The streets appeared deserted at night, when we walked in that area; photography was forbidden, though it is probable that cameras were trained on us.

Returning home for the night, we passed a neighboring apartment high-rise where Etihad flight attendants, slender, coiffed, and dressed like my vintage stewardess Barbie doll, came and went in airline shuttles at all hours. We gazed at their picture-perfect beauty. They pretty much ignored us.

⁓ː⁓

RAMADAN

Ramadan is a thirty-day period during which observant Muslims fast all day long, refraining from eating or drinking until the sun sets. It is intended as a time of spiritual focus although people are still expected to go to work and school. While it might seem like a good opportunity to regulate one's weight, it can actually lead to added girth if people break the fast with sweet dates at sunset and overindulge at Iftar.

There are only about eleven months between Ramadans. Because the lunar calendar year is shorter than the solar year, people of Muslim faith will eventually experience the holy month in every season. Insha'Allah. Summer occurrences are the most challenging since there are fewer hours without sunlight. Thus, fewer hours in which the devoted permit themselves to eat. And drink water.

University classes continue, but no one is heating anything in the faculty-lounge microwave. The coffeemaker is put away. The five-gallon cold-water dispenser is covered.

We non-Muslims paper over our office windows so we can take refreshment without being openly disrespectful, but it's pretty obvious what we're up to.

HENNA PARTY

"You're invited to a henna party," my husband told me.

Henna. When my mother was expecting me, friends told her to put henna on her hair to restore the vitality sapped by my nine months of development.

Having seen intricate reddish-brown designs on the hands of women in India and the Emirates, I knew the dye was also used for temporary tattoos on special occasions. What shall I wear to such an event? Jeans and a T-shirt? Am I liable to get brown dye on my clothes?

Emirati colleagues laughed and explained, No, you go to a salon and get the henna applied before the party. They acknowledged, though, that my understanding had some basis in historical tradition: as part of a multi-day wedding celebration, a group of women would apply elaborate patterns of bronze-colored paste to the bride's hands.

In the back room of a little salon, a young Indian woman worked a thick, rust crème into swirls and blossoms on my hands. After it set, she wiped off the excess, and I admired the orange decorations. After a few days, the dye darkens, the artist told me. Just in time for the party. Then it fades over a couple of weeks. I was hoping it would last until I got back to America.

The bride-to-be was a former student of John's. The bridegroom was one of her cousins.

Marrying of first-cousins is a longstanding tradition in much of the Middle East. Most observers would say this practice occurs due to shared values and traditions. The more cynical might say it's for pragmatic or economic reasons.

Salma had almost graduated from college when her mother announced one day that a young man was considering proposing marriage to her. Fawaz.

"I laughed," she recalled. "He was a cousin. This must be a joke."

The inquiry was sincere.

As Fawaz and his family were from Dubai and he was several years older, Salma really did not know him. Didn't recall having met him even though he remembered seeing her and falling in love immediately.

"If he were one of my local cousins, I'd never have considered a proposal," she said. "I played with them as a child, and they seem like brothers to me."

Betrothed cousins were required to undergo extensive blood testing to reveal chances of congenital birth anomaly. In cases of high potential, the couple might not wed or might be denied some forms of medical-care funding. That practice addressed the medical concerns but not the complex interrelations of extended families.

"Does it seem risky?" I asked the bride. "Marrying within the family?"

"There are always risks," she responded with a smile, and I wasn't sure we were talking about medical perspectives only.

Salma's marrying of Fawaz was not a foregone conclusion.

"Ultimately, it's your choice," the young woman's mother told her. "You don't have to marry him." Her parents did think, however, that Fawaz was a good man. They had detected how well he treated his mother and grandmother. "If you are not good to your family, you will not be good to strangers," they said.

The courtship process was unrushed. To start with, there were many phone calls between the two. They were to get acquainted and explore whether they had common interests and attitudes. The two discussed education and careers, religious perspectives, likes and dislikes. On one call Fawaz told Salma he hoped he could someday take her shopping and help choose fashions for her. (She noted years later that he never fulfilled this intention and wondered if any husband would do so.)

In another conversation, she told him she was taking driver's education classes and was excited about getting a license. He hinted that maybe the two of them could sneak off somewhere and he could teach her to drive his new Mitsubishi Lancer EX. She declined.

"My parents would disapprove," she said, "and I don't do things behind their back."

He later told her it was a good thing she had answered that way. "If you had been willing to defy your parents," he said, "I wouldn't have married you."

***

The henna party was an elaborate affair attended by five hundred people. Ladies only. Family members and friends of all ages were beautifully dressed, coiffed, and bejeweled. As each woman entered the grand ballroom, she removed her abaya and hung it on one of the coatracks by the door. The evening gown she wore would be jewel-colored satin or chiffon, with gemstones at the neckline. *Oh là là*, those necklines. Voluptuous women, heavily made up with red lips and kohl around their dark eyes, dressed in dramatic décolleté. They mingled, laughed, and enjoyed the sumptuous multi-course dinner.

Several former teachers of the bride sat at the same table as I, enjoying the carefully prepared meal and watching the festivities. Thanks to a loan from a colleague of John's, I was appropriately dressed in a bright-pink evening gown with a matching shawl.

The host family toured the perimeter of the room graciously on a carpeted runway, greeting the many well-wishers. The bride's garb, custom-made in Oman, was enchanting. Her outfit was a suit in shades of dusty blue and silver with slim, silky trousers and a brocade tunic. A long, sheer veil glittered at the edges. To this Westerner, the ensemble was reminiscent of the Victorian court dress favored by the musical artist Prince. In a good way.

Elaborate headgear showcased the bride's long, black hair. A medallion graced her forehead, and a four-tiered silver necklace was draped at her throat. She had bangles on both wrists and several fingers. Makeup had been lavishly but professionally applied. Lipstick and nail polish coordinated with stage decorations that included mirrors as well as flowing garlands of cream- and magenta-hued bougainvillea.

Later in the evening, an announcement was made, which I did not understand, and many of the elegant ladies went over to the coatracks to put their abayas back on. Most, but not all, of the women quickly concealed their designer gowns and upswept hairdos. *Is it time to go home?* Some of the female guests remained as they were: fancy, beautiful, colorful. All remained in the room.

The broad double doors to the ballroom opened, and in trooped a dozen men. A welcoming party consisting of the bridegroom with some of his family had arrived. They accompanied him to the dais where the bride waited quietly on a tufted white-velvet loveseat. The groom sat beside her for a few minutes. No vows were said. No papers were signed. No champagne toast was offered. That had happened the week before. (Contract signing, not champagne.) Only a few close family members witnessed the legal procedure, called *milcha*. Keeping a low profile is said to help avoid the gaze of the evil eye.

After a while the men departed to rejoin male festivities in another room. Some of the older, more-conservative Muslim women, having paid their respects, departed at this point. The other guests removed their abayas and hung them back on the racks. Music began to play, and the hundreds of remaining friends gradually formed a long, happy line lacing around the aisles between tables. They danced with abandon.

FEEL GREAT HELPING

The Emirates are only about 11 percent Emirati. Everyone else is there to provide services that support the new Emirati way of life in a country just fifty-five years old. Guest workers come from India, Pakistan, Bangladesh, Egypt, Philippines, Iran, and Jordan, as well as the United Kingdom, Europe, and the Americas. They work in high-tech consulting. Education. Healthcare. Finance and commerce. Construction. Tourism and hospitality. Domestic services.

Among the educators were Lorina and her husband from Canada. We two couples had dinner together occasionally in Abu Dhabi, sometimes outdoors at a golf course where she was an avid player. She sang with a chorus and was a devoted stray-cat rescuer. A librarian by profession, Lorina was interested in culture, travel, and everything else. She would take me to events like the annual Abu Dhabi Art Fair and places like the Emirati Heritage Village and Masdar City. The last is a site developing zero-emission transportation and energy-efficient building designs. Engineers are pioneering advanced solar-power integration, a natural fit in a desert that boasts nearly 3,600 hours of sunshine a year.

It was easy to enjoy fine dining and sightseeing in the UAE. Sand dunes. Beaches. Shopping malls. Visits with fellow expatriates. Most white-collar guest workers did those things. Lorina was willing to dig deeper, to get involved in other communities. She joined an army of women whose uniform was a colorful T-shirt with a pink-heart logo: Feel Great Helping. She introduced me to them.

The group had formed a few years earlier to support female immigrants who worked as retail cashiers, waiters, and domestics. Coming from overpopulated, impoverished countries, they were able to earn wages in the UAE and send remittances to families back home. Working six days a week, they led humble lives with little time or money for niceties.

Thus, the mission of Feel Great Helping was to bring a bit of brightness to the lives of some of these hard-toiling women. Not with cash. Sometimes with favorite grocery items or toiletries. But mostly with clothing or a special event: a meal in the food court of a mall, or an afternoon of folk dancing. Tea and sweets or a tour of a mosque. Maybe even a few hours at a bowling alley.

One thing that impressed me, in my limited interaction with the group, was that efforts were not scattered, one-time offerings. The FGH social network was established and strategically run by a woman with considerable business-management experience. Her organization would identify a community of women living in a workers' compound and more or less adopt them for consistent, regular contact.

The recipients living in dormitory-like labor villages didn't get bags of old, wrinkled hand-me-downs. They got dresses and blouses that were becoming to them and shoes that fit. The clothing was indeed donated, but it came from wealthy donors who had nice things to share. In the FGH leader's multi-story apartment were two rooms dedicated to this project. In one room, practical clothing. In another, luxury evening wear: gleaming satins and sequins and lace. There were nice handbags. Cosmetic products. Stacks of shoes, clean and well heeled. Literally.

The fancier pieces, nearly new, sometimes with price tags still on them, would be sold through more upscale venues. The resulting income paid for events and outings. The regular outfits would be distributed directly to the expat workers or offered at rummage sales.

I had the chance to volunteer at one of those fundraisers and to attend one of the women's outings. The social network lived up to its name, giving people the intrinsic satisfaction found in making others a little happier. Feel Great Helping wasn't going to lift any of these women out of the class of working poor. It wasn't going to buy them passage back home or send them to college. It was able to pull a few people out of the mass of nameless service workers once in a while and show them they were valued individuals.

VIETNAM

A SERIOUS VACATION

When you go on a major trip halfway around the world and your plans include a cruise, people assume you're going to enjoy a lavish escape. Visiting Vietnam and Cambodia, however, was more like life itself: some beauty and joy, some pain and sorrow, but a deeply enriching experience.

True to its reputation, Vietnam offered an absorbing adventure. But when friends ask if it was relaxing or recreational, it's hard to know how to respond. It was intense. There is so much that is serious and thought-provoking in a culture with such a turbulent past. Can we say it was fun?

Our tour planners were well aware that most of their passengers were from the United States. The guides were conscientious, hospitable, responsive, and responsible. They were also unflinching in exposing us to their pain and the aftermath of a war that clouds their history. A conflict the Vietnamese refer to as the American War.

So, while we appreciated the fields and jungles, the islands and temples, we were exposed as well to sobering reminders of historic harms suffered.

ON STREETS OF HANOI

It's Christmas, but your loved ones have moved across the country, around the world, or into eternity. When the holidays aren't what they used to be, overseas travel can be a welcome escape. If there are traditional activities you miss, or would prefer to miss, go away for a while.

***

One such year, my husband and I elected to spend a month in Vietnam and Cambodia. Lots of Buddhist temples there but no Christmas except for fake trees in hotel lobbies and Bing Crosby music in the elevators.

Before we arrived, our friend Professor Nguyen had developed a Hanoi itinerary for us. To start the week, he and his wife introduced us to cousins including a teenaged girl who gave us copies of note cards she had painted with original designs. Both families accompanied us in an open-air taxi to the seven-hundred-year-old Bat Trang pottery village on the Red River banks, southeast of Hanoi. It's a place we would never have found on our own. There we saw more than one young woman standing on a stool to hand-paint birds and garlands and apply three-dimensional clay flowers onto a seven-foot-tall vase (perhaps more appropriately called a *vahz*).

These urns would be moved into kilns the size of walk-in refrigerators, fired, then sold for thousands of dollars and transported around the world. The different steps of pottery-making took place on three levels of a narrow building. We were invited to access each floor by means of a treacherous circular stairway. I could hardly manage my own balance let alone think of carrying valuable fragilities up and down.

Hanoi is packed with nine million people and seven million motorcycles. Bikes at every intersection are overwhelming. Male or female riders, they won't run you over, but don't hesitate. Make eye contact to let them know you're stepping off the curb... *right... now!*

Our retired teacher friend was eager for us to visit the Temple of Literature. Before French colonists filled streets with their houses and administrative offices, ochre-colored and outfitted with wrought iron, this historical university was here. Eight hundred years ago, this park was established to honor education, contemplation, and literacy. Today teenagers about to complete school gather in little swarms to get graduation pictures taken. Boys in blue robes. Girls in white gowns or jewel-toned velvet dresses and impractical shoes.

Trees a hundred feet tall make the temple a relaxing center of quiet in the bustling city. Especially remarkable are the banyan trees. They appear as clusters of woody trunks; a closer inspection reveals these branches to be aerial roots that twist across the lawn, interconnecting like sculptures.

A key feature of the temple grounds is a covered porch displaying stone tablets inscribed with the names of a thousand scholars who passed imperial exams as far back as the fifteenth century. The hand-carved stelae are five feet tall and a foot thick. Each one is supported by an intricately carved stone tortoise of similar mass. The eighty-two reptilian pedestals symbolize longevity and wisdom. Turtles all the way across.

It's reassuring to honor education eight hundred miles from the killing fields of Cambodia, where Pol Pot had millions of people executed and thrown into thousands of mass graves shortly after the Vietnam War. The victims' chief crime was that they were educated. Speakers of foreign languages. Intellectuals.

Our friend claims not to be religious, but in an exhibition room of the Vietnam Fine Arts Museum, he was keen to point out the notable seventeenth-century Bodhisattva of Compassion. The lacquered wood figure represents the thousand arms and eyes of Avalokiteshvara. This particular sculpture may only have forty-two limbs, but that's enough to have one pair of hands at rest, one pair folded in prayer, and a whole bunch left for seeing and helping all the suffering beings of the world.

Along the sidewalks of Hanoi, informal café owners were scrubbing dishes and pots and pans on the sidewalk, using garden hoses that drained into the open gutters. The colorful tables and chairs of these informal eateries quickly vanished from sight when police approached.

On one of our afternoons together, our informal guide invited us to have the Obama special for lunch at a café where the U.S. President had dined with chef Anthony Bourdain in 2016. Their little table and tiny plastic chairs are preserved behind glass, always camera-ready.

It was obligatory to enjoy an egg coffee at some point, and we managed to do this before departing Hanoi. The eponymously named beverage consists of Vietnamese robusta topped with a froth of whipped egg yolk and sweetened condensed milk. Velvety smooth and soothing.

***

By the time you get back from your international flight, your own home with its western automobiles and architecture will seem like a foreign place. The only remnants of the holidays recently celebrated here will be scattered bits of pine needles and some tinsel that fell to the pavement next to the green, wheeled trash cans. As the weeks go by, you'll have the vague feeling you missed something. As if the calendar had a circadian rhythm and this year it was slightly askew.

⁓ I ⁓

TUNNEL RATS

Landmines, like animosity, remain in a land long after overt warfare has ceased. Buried explosives kill and maim civilians, hindering the agricultural and industrial development needed to return to normalcy and increase productivity.

A Belgian Buddhist monk with an engineering background developed the idea of teaching rodents to train their keen sense of smell on the distinct scents of certain explosives.

What a peace-loving undertaking.

A nonfiction book in a series designed to strengthen primary-school reading skills, *Hero Rats,* tells of large, specially trained rodents that can sniff out unexploded ordnance. They have been used in Mozambique, Cambodia, and other parts of Africa and Asia for signaling humans to defuse landmines rather than be destroyed by them.

The children's reader does not tell about the human soldiers known as tunnel rats. These were men who disarmed trap wires and landmines. In Vietnam, they engaged in combat within the claustrophobic burrows that measured as narrow as 24 by 29 inches. The fighters were brave but small: no one taller than 5-feet-5-inches could navigate within them. Originating during Japanese occupation of the country in the 1940s, the tunnels eventually extended some 155 miles. The labyrinths were extensive and ingeniously designed. They included an extensive network that connected barracks, kitchens, training rooms, hospitals, and storage units. Air ducts were disguised by termite hills. Small amounts of smoke could be released through multiple remote exits so that smoldering tendrils were barely noticeable. Viet Cong soldiers could stay for weeks in the dark burrows that laced through the jungle.

Most American and Australian soldiers couldn't even fit into the underground channels, let alone traverse through them for mile after mile. Those who did so were subject to all manner of traps, such as dead ends and reversed-claw spikes that prevented them from either progressing or backing out, so they suffocated.

How could conventional western armies ever have hoped to win a war fought in such circumstances?

I'd been to more than one notorious Holocaust concentration camp in Europe, but I balked at the opportunity to examine every instrument of torture in the outdoor museum displays of Vietnam. We did visit the Cu Chi Tunnels northwest of Ho Chi Minh City (Saigon), which serve as a much-visited memorial with seventy-five miles of tunnels maintained intact. A few hardy visitors in our cohort accepted the challenge of descending into a tunnel and crouching their way twenty yards underground to the next exit. Another tourist tried to fit into a hole widened after the war, thought better of it, and backed out.

How do you climb into the air-conditioned tour bus, return to your luxury hotel, and prepare for a sumptuous evening banquet at the end of a day like that?

A RELIGIOUS EXPERIENCE

In the midst of so many challenges to happiness in Vietnam, numerous Zen principles were presented on this trip. Our tour guide, Dang, exemplified a Buddhist philosophy of life. The young man had already endured a postwar childhood and had recently been diagnosed with cancer. Yet he daily encouraged us, the twenty travelers in his charge, to focus on appreciation, to breathe deeply, to clear our minds of distractions, and to live in the moment. Every moment.

He sent each of us home with a little white Buddha perched on a green-onyx base to set somewhere in our houses where we'd be sure to see it every day. Mine sits among the philodendrons on a dining-room window sill, smiling pacifically in the morning sun. It's a sweet, inspiring reminder.

But I am the least Zen-like person. My internal dialogue is full of wishes and worries:

Will my family be safe on the highway today? Did I do a good job writing that recommendation letter? What if the neighbors don't like my potato salad?

"How is this going to work?" I wondered when Dang proposed to take us to a temple for a blessing. As I consider myself Christian, I was unsure how to approach this Buddhist activity. Should I observe or participate? What could I get out of it? What should I take from it?

We were told to remove our shoes and hats (to have our heads *uncovered*) when we entered the temple. Two monks with shaved heads and maroon robes sat cross-legged before the group. We were requested to assume a similar pose or, if we couldn't manage that, to sit such that we were not exposing our feet toward the altar.

The young men, teenagers yet, scattered flower petals. A bell rang. They started chanting. I closed my eyes. How shall I spend this quiet time productively? I'll pray for people I'm concerned about. The usual list formed on my lips, starting my customary bedtime ritual. In the mystical temple setting, loved ones' images began appearing vividly in my mind's eye, one after another. Mother, Ann, Tanja, Jan... old Bob Merkley, my uncle's magician friend with the Coke-bottle eyeglasses. Goodness, where did he come from? I hadn't thought of him in years. It was like a slideshow of connections in deep enamel colors. One after the other, unsummoned. More names, more cherished kin. Warm tones, faces close-up and smooth, expressions serene.

Mesmerized, I must have begun to lean to one side because someone touched me, and I had to regain my balance. Lapsing easily back into a trance, I was able to descend into peacefulness until the chanting ended and the bells rang again. All too soon. Bringing me back to daylight and the material world. To the presence of people around me. To standing up and steadying myself. No time to be alone and ponder the unique experience.

INDIA

MUMBAI: GATEWAY OF INDIA

Shritik suggested John should be his porter when he returned to India. A big white guy toting the little Indian man's baggage around for him. Having left humble family circumstances in Mumbai fifty years earlier to pursue a doctorate and become a professor in America, our colleague quite liked this imagined role reversal.

When Shritik was unable to accompany us, we went to India on our own and visited friends of his. Prisha and her husband Vihaan met us at the airport in the evening. We followed them outside, where scores of men sat on squares of cardboard, not so much begging as living there.

Across town, our friends' apartment was on the fourth floor. It had three bedrooms, one of which was completely dedicated to their favorite god, the elephant-headed Ganesha. They said they were grateful for the blessings they'd had in life and thought setting up this altar was an appropriate show of respect.

My clothes were sticking to me. I couldn't wait to get to their guestroom and disrobe. At night, an open upstairs window might provide a refreshing breeze, but before bedtime our hosts insisted on shutting every opening and locking it fast.

Early in the morning the bakery man made his rounds, ringing a bell on his little black *tuk-tuk* to announce his arrival with fresh breads. Prisha had appointments on her calendar and welcomed me to go with her.

In the afternoon was a baby shower. No one knew me, but everyone was welcoming. In the early evening, Prisha stopped by a doctor's office. The dermatologist offered her no treatment for her recently acquired freckles. Avoid the sun. No bleaching cream? India is famous – or infamous – for use of skin whiteners. Yet this physician suggested nothing for a bona fide skin discoloration.

On the way home from this disappointing doctor visit, Prisha walked with me to a busy open-air market just after dark. It was a lively scene where vendors were offering *vada pav* sandwiches, fresh flowers, and children's clothing.

On another afternoon, Vihaan decided we should go shopping for Indian clothing for us. Finding a *kameez* or tunic for me was fun and relatively easy. But an Indian shirt for John proved more difficult. He is decidedly bigger than the average East Indian. We stopped in a couple of narrow shops without success. The shopkeeper at the last one was more determined. When shirts on the racks did not fit, he sent an employee to a back room to look for larger sizes. The assistant did not return through the back door. Instead, a white ceiling panel shifted above the cashier's head, and a thin, brown arm reached down from the attic holding a dark-green garment in a clear plastic package. John's personal shopping assistant.

To escape the heat of the city, and give our hosts some peace for a couple of days, we booked a stay in the hill station of Matheran in the Sahyadri forest. To get there, we needed to take two trains. Worried we'd not make the connection at Neral, Vihaan took the first train, the Central Line, with us.

The train cars were packed with men. At each stop, the new on-boarders would essentially press everyone else farther into the center of the car. The trick was not to get crammed in so far that you couldn't reach the door at your destination, nor stay so close to the front that you got expelled prematurely by the exiting crowd behind you.

No one sits. You grab onto straps if you can reach one. It might not be necessary; humanity is so tightly packed in that you could probably faint and not fall over. I got separated from our host, but our fellow passengers were mindful of our otherness and propelled us along, communicating to one another on our behalf. *Gotta' help these clueless white people.*

The tracks curved to such an extent that we could see the rest of the train cars behind us. What we saw was young men literally hanging onto the outside of the train. *Ralph Nader does not live here.*

Did these commuters have train tickets? What was the fare for riding outside, clinging for dear life on your daily shuttle?

After depositing us at our connection platform, Vihaan returned home. We continued. From Neral a narrow-gauge train bore us uphill above sweeping green valleys for two more hours until we were 50 miles from Mumbai and 2,600 feet higher. Hill stations were developed in the 1800s by the British, seeking a getaway from muggy summer weather. Some were used as military cantonments and feature British colonial architecture. In Matheran the roads were red from iron-rich soil. A swarm of Indian men rushed to escort us to our hotel. We hired one of these *faux guides* to keep the rest from pestering us. After helping us with our bags and asking the kitchen staff to store a vial of insulin in their refrigerator for me, the young man offered to show us the way to a lush nature path. We expected a substantial tour and explanations, but after a few minutes, he heard a whistle announcing the next trainload of tourists and abruptly abandoned us at the top of a hill.

Behind our hotel was a large, cool patio where guests lounged in the shade. From there it's amusing to sit and watch cute, lanky monkeys scampering about in strong, lofty trees. Until you get back upstairs to your room and realize your bananas are missing. I always have food with me. Nuts, crackers, fruit. The window I'd left ajar was an open invitation to tree-climbing macaques and langurs, who could scramble up a tree, enter our room, and quickly leave with their loot.

I learned my lesson, but a tourist we saw at a nearby zoo made a similar mistake. She wore her backpack into a walk-in monkey cage. Accustomed to human visitors, the little simians were clever enough to climb onto the girl's shoulders, unzip her pack, and start pulling things out. A bottle of sunscreen? *Yuck!* They tossed that to the ground. They discarded anything that wasn't edible, and grabbed the granola bars and fruit.

In the hotel courtyard we contemplated next steps, planning to visit Mani Bhavan museum and library, housed where Mahatma Gandhi lived in the early 1900s. After that a tour guide would take us to the 1,500-year-old carved-rock caves of Ajanta and the Buddhist, Hindu, and Jain caves of Ellora. Thousands of tons of rock must have been removed in the development of these cliffside temples, creating multi-level structures with detailed artwork. The walls of sixty caves are painted and carved, sometimes in high relief, creating figures that emerge from the wall like statues. When we got there, a family from Pune chatted with us, and we all took a short bus ride together. We exchanged cameras to take pictures; now our images are immortalized in the collection of someone we'll remember but never see again.

Following a couple days of relaxing in the semi-evergreen forest, we packed to return to Mumbai. I stopped at the front desk and asked the clerk to retrieve my insulin from the refrigerator in the restaurant. There it was, in its glass bottle in the original orange-and-white box. Frozen solid and therefore useless.

*

ARRANGED MARRIAGE

I attended a baby shower in India but never a wedding. However, our friends' son had married the year before we visited Mumbai. They proudly showed us a lengthy video of the ceremony and the days of events surrounding it. The parents reveled in watching it as though seeing it for the first time. "We do this often," the groom's mother said. "Sometimes in the evening when we have nothing else to do."

The home movie was filled with colorful costumes, music, and expansive trays of the various feasts that had taken place. Happy people surrounded by sparkling red and yellow decorations in fancy venues. An altar adorned with flowers. They took such delight in reliving every recorded moment.

Their son, Arjun, had always been a bright boy, and they were pleased to be able to send him to the United States for medical school. After years of study and internships, his ambitious parents urged him to stay in the States long enough to complete residencies in a field of specialization.

If these milestones were not adequate, now, they advised, it was time for Arjun to marry and start a family. Give them grandchildren. They would find a nice Indian girl for him. Well connected in their community, they were confident of securing attractive, appropriate marriage prospects to consider.

He resisted. They persisted.

Finally, the new doctor said, "All right, I'll take care of it. I can find my own wife." Within a year, he was engaged to a young American woman whose parents were from India.

Ecstatic, both sets of parents began making preparations for elaborate celebrations on two continents. Extensive invitation lists. Banquet hall rentals. An engagement party in the USA. A similar but bigger affair in India. Caterers and photographers hired. A videographer too, obviously.

Clothing was custom made suitable to each event. For the bride, extravagant saris. Half a dozen of them for the multi-day celebration. Shimmering silk and vibrant satin in brilliant pinks and reds, draped to show off fabric designs with intricate metallic embroidery. In addition to the main wedding ceremony, the bride and all the wedding party must have new clothing to wear to a Ganesh Puja prayer ritual conducted by a Hindu priest, a Mehndi night henna function, an evening of singing and dancing, and a welcoming luncheon hosted by the groom's family following the wedding day.

When we visited, months after the nuptials, Arjun's mother and father were still enjoying the afterglow of the festivities, perhaps more than the newlyweds were enjoying their honeymoon.

Arjun returned to working long hours in the medical field that had become his passion. Rotating shifts at a hospital, case notes to study at home, and publishable research conducted with a fellow scholar.

His new wife, barely out of college, had no career. She did not know his colleagues. Born and educated in America, she was not used to his traditional ideals and expectations. She did not know how to cook what he liked. Could hardly get him to talk to her in the evenings, to share her interests, to go anywhere on the weekends.

The highly accomplished young man had not wanted an arranged marriage. Had not particularly wanted a marriage at all.

A year after we sat watching their wedding video in Mumbai, the couple separated.

⁓❢⁓

PAKISTAN

WEDDING IN PESHAWAR

Advisory: The U.S. Department of State recommends that U.S. citizens "Reconsider Travel" to Pakistan due to terrorism and the potential for armed conflict. The U.S. government has limited ability to provide services to U.S. citizens...

"We're invited to a wedding in Pakistan," John announced. "My friend's getting married in Peshawar. Some of my other colleagues will be there too."

Ever pushing the limits of adventure, we accepted the invitation and began the extensive paperwork required to visit the Islamic Republic of Pakistan. Visas and formal letters of invitation, precise travel dates and destination addresses. Fees to pay and trips to embassies. Waiting periods and exchanging our currency for rupees.

As expected, there would be several events to the multi-day celebration. What shall I wear, and what should we offer as a gift?

The party was a family event, so we had the chance to meet several generations. Three attractive girls in their early teens came dressed alike, though they were not siblings. Perhaps intrigued by the foreigners, they approached me, and we exchanged information on how we knew the bridegroom.

"We are cousins."

"We are colleagues."

"What do you teach?"

"What do you study?"

Hoping to engage them in further conversation, I asked for their impressions of the wedding. "Does it make you think about getting married some day?" Banal question from an adult.

"Oh, we will get married eventually, but we want to finish our education first." Wise response from a child.

Music played, and a man insisted I get up and join the circle dance. That would not have happened in Abu Dhabi. The gentleman had no idea what an uncoordinated dancer I was, but I tried to follow the leader and stay in step with the rhythm. When they changed directions, they took me by surprise, and my main objective was to stay on my feet. We all laughed.

***

A smaller reception took place at the home of a family member. In a pleasant neighborhood, far from the gray and dusty roads of town, the white house was enclosed by a wall with a tall, iron gate. When we arrived, our driver was unable to open the gate. Inside we heard a scuffle and the sound of something banging against metal. These could not be signs of a brawl, as no alcohol would be consumed here.

The driver advised us to wait a couple of minutes until things were calm. When we got inside and passed through the courtyard, we saw a big pool of blood on the concrete. A goat had been ceremonially sacrificed in gratitude to Allah for the nuptials. It would not become our dinner; it was to be donated to the poor. So I felt gratitude as well.

⁓!⁓

MISSTEPS IN PAKISTAN

*"But the worst thing I've ever done... this was horrible...
I never felt so bad in my entire life..."*
~ Chunk, *The Goonies*

Edith Piaf belted out her signature anthem, "Non, je ne regrette rien!" If we are to believe biographies written about the singer's colorful career in the World War II era and her connections with this song, Piaf never looked back on misdeeds in her life. I wish I could say the same: that I have no regrets. A thousand do-overs might begin to erase the subjects of my self-recriminations.

One of my worst foreign missteps related to the marriage in Pakistan. A colleague's wedding invitation beckoned us to visit, for the first time, a country with the U.S. Department of Defense "Do Not Travel" designation. We really did intend to behave ourselves discretely and fly under the radar.

The destination was a slight bit daring, thus prompting us to call upon our familiar refrain, "The adventure begins." Moving to Europe. Going to Egypt. Quitting our jobs to attend graduate school. Even trips to the hospital for surgery. We said it the morning we stepped aboard a plane for our flight to Islamabad. *The adventure begins.*

The bridegroom's best man met John and me at the airport. On the drive from Islamabad to Peshawar, we stopped at a fuel station and stepped into a small convenience store. As I was getting back into the car, I overheard our host telling strangers that we were visitors from Canada. He drove us onto a small military base, where he stopped to show credentials. His car pulled up to the front porch of the guesthouse. Inside the tiny front office, conversations and paperwork took place without our understanding a word. Up narrow stairs, we found a spacious room decorated in maroon and gold. A window overlooked the front patio and some of the buildings in the compound. Lovely. We were going to be so comfortable here. Rafiq left us, saying we should take a rest and await his phone call later in the afternoon concerning dinner plans.

First order of business in a hotel is not napping or unpacking or checking if there's anything on TV. It's my husband's orientation ritual, taking the measure of the city. In this case, the cantonment. We went downstairs, and the official at the desk inquired in limited English if we needed something. We said we would like to go outside and walk around. He looked doubtful.

"Maybe we just walk around the perimeter of the camp? Or go across to that other building?" He said something we did not understand and indicated a soccer field. That's precisely where we went: around the fenced-in court where two men were practicing soccer. I had dressed modestly and covered my head with a colorful shayla John's students had given me. We nodded hello and received no acknowledgment, but the larger man watched us carefully on our short outing.

After we returned to our room, Rafiq called. He wanted to come and pick us up. So soon? Yes, please come downstairs now. Bring your luggage.

In the car, Rafiq said we needed to find different lodging. We learned that we should not have been walking about the compound and should especially have stayed away from the football field.

After some distance, our driver turned into a narrow alleyway lined with tall cement walls that led into a dark, underground facility. Rugged-looking men admitted us, and we were led down a dim hallway to a tiny, dark room. We brought our suitcases in, but John later told the groom that I was afraid there. It felt like a hostage dungeon.

After a few more hours, Rafiq took us to another place, a light and bright multi-story hotel painted a welcoming yellow with parking spaces outside and normal-looking guests. It did, however, have chain-link fencing all around the grounds, and throughout the week we noticed various nicely dressed men loitering in the lobby or pacing in the front courtyard. They were not threatening but did not seem to have much to do other than keep an eye on us.

What an ignorant thing we had done. I am still ashamed at the trouble we caused in the midst of a festive and complexly orchestrated weekend of events.

Years later, the groom visited us in America, and recalled the incident. I told him how mortified I still felt. He laughed and said that what had seemed a nightmare at the time had later become an anecdote he enjoyed retelling.

~I~

JORDAN

PETRA, NOT PALESTINE

We've known Abdel for several decades, since our grad-school days at Syracuse University. He was one of twenty Humphrey Fellows in a Fulbright program for journalists. We've kept in touch all that time. Though we've traveled in dozens of countries, my husband and I have never been able to visit Abdel and his family. They live in Palestine.

One year the couple proposed meeting in Jordan over the holidays. We agreed on Sweimeh on the eastern shore of the Dead Sea.

We exchanged gifts; I still treasure the handmade, woven black-and-red scarf and matching needlepoint jewelry. Given that our friends are Muslim, I thought it was open-minded and big-hearted of them also to offer ceramic souvenirs from Jerusalem such as a Christian tourist might choose.

Our families went together on a tour to the Jordan River, near where Jesus is believed to have been baptized by, yes, John the Baptist! A tour van took us all up to Mount Nebo, where tradition holds that Moses viewed the Promised Land before his death. Another afternoon we lounged in Ma'in hot springs at a scenic spot in the mountains. Its waterfalls reach as hot as 140 degrees Fahrenheit. Relaxing in a gender-segregated pool allowed me some time to get acquainted with Abdel's wife, whom I'd never met but felt I had known for many years.

In the evening, conversation turned to regional politics. Our friends gave us a more thorough understanding of their life situation. Previously, I had imagined the Palestinian West Bank and Israel interface to be something like Berlin after World War II: a solid barrier between two distinctly divided segments. Abdel's descriptions of daily life sent me to study the map. Arab areas were separated and divided into many enclaves. There was no Checkpoint Charlie, no single gate or barrier to movement. There were hundreds. Some were temporary, so you never knew when your day's duties and errands might be delayed by stops and inspections. Our friend once scheduled surgery after months of waiting for an available date, only to be barred from entering the designated hospital in another part of town when the appointed day came.

When conflicts flared, whether skirmishes or outright war, tempers flared too.

"My younger children are frightened," Abdel told us, "and my older sons are angry."

There was little we could do to help. We offered for one of their children to come to the USA to study, but that never came to pass.

The day after our friends returned to the West Bank, John and I went down to the water. You can't go home without a picture of yourself floating effortlessly in (or on) the sea.

"I can't swim."

You don't have to; you will float. If you can relax enough. Other tourists are simultaneously encouraging me and laughing at me. It's most effective to lie down, if you don't mind getting your hair in the saltwater. Otherwise position yourself like you're sitting, legs straight out in front of you, and you'll find yourself floating.

This is not the time to show off your favorite new swimsuit. In addition to becoming encrusted in saline, you'll have mud all over yourself and your bathing suit from the obligatory application of the local skin treatment. Dark, sticky, gray-brown mud from a community barrel on the shore. The Dead Sea is 34 percent salt, nine times saltier than ocean water, so no complex life can survive there. However, the mud is rich in minerals including sulfur, and people from all over the world go to the Dead Sea for relief from inflammation and a range of skin ailments.

***

Following the rare and precious rendezvous with our friends, John and I proceeded to Petra. The Rose City is one of the Wonders of the World and a UNESCO World Heritage Site. A commercial center was developed there by nomadic Arabs three hundred years before Christ. The Nabataeans traded spices and incense along caravan routes linking Arabia, Egypt, and Mesopotamia. Two thousand years later, a million visitors a year go there to admire structures carved into pink sandstone hills.

Several days in a row, we caught a ride from our hotel in Wadi Musa down the hill to the Petra entrance. From there, a one-mile walk took us through a narrow, winding gorge called the Siq. It's a thrill to stand in front of the edifice used as the Grail Temple in an *Indiana Jones* film. This is Al-Khazneh, "The Treasury." Scholars say it was a mausoleum or royal tomb carved into a sandstone cliff face 2,000 years ago.

Music runs through my mind. *Da, ta-ta-daaa, da-ta-da, da-daaaa!*

The opening to the Siq passage needs one of those red-and-white international signs for "do not." A red-and-white circle with a slash, as featured in the *Ghostbusters* movie logo.

It should read, "No Indy!" to keep people from humming theme song "The Raiders March."

Instead, there's a sign by the post where tourists can rent camels or donkeys. It's a humane-society plea targeted at hefty Americans: "Hey, John, get off that poor, little donkey! You're too big for him." My spouse tried not to take it personally. We were planning to go on foot (our own feet) anyway, even up to ed-Deir, the monastery high on a hill.

New Year's Eve began as an overcast day, and as we walked toward Petra, the wind picked up. We soldiered on, glad to have brought lightweight jackets. By afternoon, snow was coming down, subduing the Petra color palette.

That was a particularly strenuous day, so we decided to accept a return ride offered by our innkeeper. We called, and he said he would drive to us. We started walking. After some time, he rang back to say he could not reach us, as the streets were blocked, and he had tried alternate routes with no success. That was curious. We kept walking.

It was getting dark when we heard loud voices up ahead. Holiday revelers? We kept going, along the narrow sidewalk; around a corner, the disturbance grew louder. There seemed to be a bonfire in the middle of the road. The air began to smell like burning rubber. We soon saw that a luxury motorcoach parked in front of a tourist hotel was in flames. A crowd was rioting.

We started coughing. Our eyes started burning, and our throats scratched. *What—?*

It's tear gas!

As we stumbled forward, covering our faces, someone called to us from inside a small restaurant, and we were taken into the bathroom to splash our faces with cool water. It seemed advisable to stay off the streets for a while, so John and I joined a dozen young backpackers at a table and had a cool drink. One young woman said she worked for a nonprofit organization in Afghanistan and lived in one of many repurposed train shipping containers. They were stacked two-high, and she had a "top floor" unit that swayed gently in any strong wind. Two young people who appeared to be a couple were from different nations and had met each other online through a trekkers' website. Another couple was comprised of a guy from England and a woman from Spain. Their friendliness and adventurous spirit were a refreshing part of that day.

Our new friends began to make their way to their hostels. Still, our driver could not come. A restaurant employee advised we were not far from our hotel; he would indicate a quiet back road to take. Then he decided he should accompany us.

At our hotel, the innkeeper apologized for the civil disruption: "It has nothing to do with foreign tourists," he assured us. "The burning tour bus was empty."

Returning to the Petra archaeological site the next day, we browsed the merchant tents and tables. John decided to ask one shop owner if he knew anything about trouble in the village the preceding night.

The shopkeeper knew more than he wished he did. During the previous year, a high-profile businessman had been making lots of money and helping local investors get wealthy too. This new company was dealing in real estate and automobiles. Shareholders could profit from the sales of land and luxury cars. The shopkeeper's father kept urging him to invest. He'd held back, been skeptical. Fortunes were being made all around them. Father became insistent. Son relented. Just before the operation collapsed and was revealed to be an unsustainable Ponzi scheme. Cars were being sold and delivered, but only the earliest purchasers got what they paid for. In later cases, ownership titles never materialized. Vehicles were repossessed and sold again. New money quit coming in, so investment returns stopped.

To make matters worse, the swindlers had been permitted to slip out of town quickly and quietly. What enraged the townspeople that New Year's Eve was that local officials had protected the criminals from facing any consequences. The tourist bus was simply collateral damage.

※

TURKEY

TAXIS IN TURKEY

East meets West in the Bosphorus Strait. We meet east and west in Istanbul. In the airport, I can't help noticing that my husband can't help noticing a pretty young woman with thick black hair, a brown mini-skirted suit, and high heels. She's smiling and running across the arrival terminal. Not toward us but straight into the welcome embrace of a sturdy older woman clothed head to toe in dull, gray robe and headscarf. Past meets future.

The plane approach and landing have been rough, and I can't wait to get to our hotel, where I hope to relax and wash up. Straight away, I plug in my portable teapot, planning to boil some water to brush my teeth. *Zap!* The room lights go out. We stand very still; maybe they'll self-correct. They don't. We stumble in the dark for switches, which do nothing. We might have to alert the front desk. John opens the door to peer down the hall. No lights there either. No lights anywhere. Thanks to my little western device and my obsession with microbes, I have managed to blow a fuse that shuts down power to the whole floor.

A day later, as we walk in town, two adolescent Turkish girls in short skirts approach us on the broken sidewalk.

"Auntie, auntie!" As a woman, I am more approachable to them than John is. The teens ask if we will answer a survey. Yes, of course. The main question concerns European Union accession and whether we, as Americans, believe their country is qualified and ready for admission. We give the affirmative response we know will please them. During this entire transaction, a few yards away, a grandma in traditional garb has been watching us carefully.

True to form, John has studied the relevant *DK Eyewitness Guide*. By the time we reach Istanbul, he has a list of churches and church ruins to visit. Of course, we'll go to the massive Blue Mosque with its high-gloss Iznik tile work hand-painted in florals and geometrics of brilliant turquoise, cobalt, and red. We'll muse at the twenty-four-foot calligraphic *roundel* medallions suspended in Hagia Sophia, which has been an Orthodox Christian cathedral, a mosque, and a museum. Naturally, we will see famous Topkapi Palace and walk along sections of the Theodosian Walls with their guard towers and fortified gates. Inspect the ruins of the Church of Saint John of Studius. Visit the Chora Church/Mosque.

However, less-travelled sites have even greater appeal. We hire a taxi for the day, and the driver plans our route. He speaks no English, but John shows him our desired destinations in the book, and he indicates that he knows where most of these places are.

Church of Saint Mary of the Mongols. Greek Orthodox since its inception.

Church of Saint Stephen of the Bulgars. Bulgarian Orthodox as opposed to Greek Orthodox Patriarchate.

Church of the Pammakaristos, filled with Byzantine mosaics. A pre-Ottoman structure later converted to a mosque.

Church of the Pantocrator. Also transformed into a mosque.

Mosque of Selim I. Actually built to be a mosque.

In a small, quiet Greek Orthodox church, we are welcomed by the priest who dons his vestments and says a formal blessing for me.

At each stop, our driver knows where to park, and he waits for us while we enter churches and mosques. The last one on the list is an obscure little place down some unknown alley. The driver has never heard of this one, so he stops and asks directions. Another short ride, and he pulls over to a curb. Using not a word of English, he gives John an idea of how he might walk to it.

"You wait here. I'll run ahead and see if I can find it," John decides. My partner and protector bolts from the car and disappears into some shadowy warren. In the backseat I sit quietly for a while. A long while. My husband is taking longer than I expected. A man approaches from inside a dimly lit shop. He looks at me in the backseat. I try to hide behind my long blond hair.

Now the driver gets out of the car and follows the man into the store. In the shadows I see him consulting with the swarthy shopkeeper. Following his exchange with this stranger, the driver jumps back into the car, starts the motor, pulls away from the curb, and speeds away up a hill. John is nowhere in sight. He'll never be able to find me now. The driver continues for a few blocks. He turns a corner.

Oh, Lord! Help me! I'm going to be kidnapped and sold into white slavery.

Before my panic can reach full peak, the cabbie pulls over and stops.

Oh. Whew! It's not about human trafficking. He was looking for a legal parking spot.

KOSOVO

NEWBORN

NEWBORN. The typographic monument in the center of Pristina consists of the single English-language word in big block letters. The sculpture was unveiled in 2008, the year Kosovo officially declared its independence. The youngest country in the world. The letters were all bright yellow, the color of the stars in the European Union flag.

The painted steel structure, prominently placed in the capital city, was later repainted with the flags of the countries that had officially recognized Kosovo. The political statement was colorful. Inspiring. Clever. Splashy in its display of international emblems. Subtle in its omission of nations that were not recognizing Kosovan independence.

When I was there years later, the monument was adorned with a motif centered on climate change. Each letter of the word "NEWBORN" featured a different theme related to global warming, such as biodiversity, recycling, or water. The design was one of many temporary transformations that the tribute undergoes each year to reflect current aspirations.

The little country is no longer the newest in the world. It is no longer newborn but perhaps adolescent. It awaits emancipation into the adulthood of full worldwide recognition.

LULJETA'S KOSOVO

One morning, Luljeta's father met a cousin in town. This relative told him: "I'm struggling financially. Can you help me?" Her father answered, "For God's sake, I don't have any cash right now, but I have two cows. Take one and sell it, and whenever God gives you the chance, you can pay me back." That afternoon, the cousin coincidentally ran into Luljeta's mother. He also asked her for money. Completely unaware of the earlier encounter, she gave an equivalent response: "You may have one of our two cows."

Luljeta likes to tell this story because, she says, it reflects not just her parents' character but a generous attitude that is prevalent throughout the culture. It's one of the things she loves most about Kosovo: that people are charitable even in poverty.

(The cousin later admitted that he was not in need and had only asked the question to see how they would respond. Whether that is also typically Kosovar behavior, Luljeta didn't say.)

To meet Luljeta is to encounter an attractive young professional. She's nicely dressed and has a white-collar job. She's even-tempered with a peaceful, friendly spirit. You'd never know how her father had sacrificed for his children's education and died too soon. You wouldn't guess that she'd suffered a childhood of war trauma and deprivation. Unless perhaps you knew she was born in Kosovo in the early 1990s.

One of eight siblings, Luljeta was five years old at the start of the Kosovo War of 1998-99. Unlike many neighbor families who left the country at that time, they stayed.

"We went through many days without food, shivering from the cold, sleeping in abandoned buildings without doors or windows, or even out in the fields."

By the time the conflict was over, her mother had lost her father, brother, uncle, and cousin.

"When we returned home, everything was destroyed: the house, everything was reduced to ashes. After the war, we didn't start from zero — it felt more like below zero," Luljeta said. Gradually they were able to replace many of the material losses.

Her parents valued learning so, as life got a bit easier over a few years, the children were able to attend public school in their village. However, to go to high school, they would have to take a bus into a bigger city. In that transition, the contrast between rural and urban education became evident. The city kids had been exposed to broader course options, which gave them an advantage when it came time for higher education.

While Luljeta is grateful for the education she got, she laments the uneven quality of education across the country. Many schools lack proper infrastructure, and the quality of teaching often depends on the motivation of individual teachers. Public schools emphasize rote memorization rather than creative, individual thinking. Other alternatives are expensive, including private schools, high school, and college.

"In our home, the first of September was always a celebration," Luljeta recalled. On that date, her father would take his salary and come home with scores of notebooks and all the other supplies they might need for the whole year. He would announce, "I'm buying everything at once, so you can't say, 'I won't study because I don't have this or that.'"

"We kept those books carefully and shared them among ourselves."

Paying for supplies and transportation for four high schoolers at once was an expensive proposition, but it enabled all of the children to go to college. When three siblings were at university at the same time, their father took on the extra job of selling firewood in order to afford the fees. Ultimately, all eight kids completed bachelor's studies, and some even attained master's degrees. One of the older sisters was working while studying. Every week she shared some of her earnings.

"This was how families managed: those who came to study in the city would support the younger siblings who were just starting," she said.

Even with college diplomas, meaningful positions are hard to come by. The economy is growing, but unemployment remains high due to the still-emerging market economy and, some would say, to corruption.

"You can study hard and work hard; it's still very challenging to secure a good job," Luljeta said. "When it comes to public-sector jobs, those feel almost unreachable."

Many Kosovars, possibly too many, choose degrees in law, economics, or political science, thinking these disciplines are prestigious or will lead to government work. It is not clear that jobs are available in these fields. The enrollment of students in "exact sciences" such as chemistry, physics, or biology has declined dramatically, which handicaps a society needing infrastructure development and modernization. Increasing numbers of young Kosovars want to leave their country. Attracted by the life they perceive through the Internet, they imagine they'll find better opportunities internationally.

As the country creeps forward, some wounds are being covered over without healing. Today's young adults remember being homeless and hungry as small children during the Kosovo War. They cannot forget the people and homes they lost. Some older adults fear that the next generation will not be interested in the war, in pursuing justice for war crimes, or in speaking Albanian.

The young country continues to make progress. Technology has connected the people to the rest of the world and changed society in many ways, most of them positive. Rural women have their own cellphones now. (Whether they can use these devices in privacy may be another matter.) Citizens and tourists enjoy events such as the FemArt fair, Sunny Hill Festival of music, and the documentary-film festival DokuFest. A recent decision called visa liberalization permits Kosovars to enter most EU countries (the Schengen area) for short stays without additional barriers.

"The biggest progress is freedom of movement and expression," Luljeta declared. "When I was a child, war and conflict shaped everything. Now, young people can dream, travel, study abroad, and return with new perspectives."

Today Luljeta is married and has a daughter. She hopes her child will grow up in a Kosovo with more opportunities to practice curiosity, critical thinking, and creativity, with an education that "opens horizons, makes her courageous, and prepares her for life."

BECOMING

Emelia had just graduated from college in the USA when I met her and her mother over lunch at a little café. She was looking for insights on international public relations in preparation for upcoming work in Kosovo. This was shortly after the war, when Kosovo Force (NATO) peacekeeping troops were reducing their presence in the country. I glanced at her mother, looking for signs of concern but saw in her a sense of adventure similar to her daughter's. So off went Emelia: a new graduate to a new country.

This would not be her first experience in Kosovo. She was a high schooler during the Kosovo War, and televised images of ethnic Albanians being forced to flee their homes made a lasting impression. Emelia was already interested in global politics, and she had a friend living in Pristina. She was interested to observe how conditions would develop and how well the United Nations might help govern a country. As soon as it was feasible, she visited the West Balkans region via a circuitous route at a time when the capital city did not have a viable airport.

That was November 2001, and her accommodations were in a basement apartment. She couldn't remember having been so cold indoors before, and she'd press the buttons on a little gas heater in her room. No one had told her not to leave it on all night because she might asphyxiate.

The first democratic elections were taking place, and the young visitor found it exciting to watch people lined up to vote. She could not enter voting halls, but she recalled a surreal experience during that election period. Her host decided they should take a drive to visit a Serbian church in a nearby valley. It was densely foggy when they noticed a car gradually emerging through the mist. Then another car and another. A caravan of official vehicles appeared to be following them. They turned out to be ballot counters, working to assure fair counting at the polls.

Emelia returned home excited about the possibilities and kept track of developments in Kosovo while she attended university. She was drawn by the idea of making a contribution to society in what was about to become the newest country in the world.

If Emelia was starting out in her career life, this Balkan land was declaring its independence too. Both were embarking on years-long challenges.

***

Challenges for Kosovo included unemployment, infrastructure, public transportation, diverse languages and cultures, and economics. And, most of all, independence because this could lead to improvements in the other areas.

Trials and tests have confronted the Republic of Kosovo since the breakup of Yugoslavia. It has struggled continuously for universal recognition of its autonomy. Meanwhile, Serbia continues to consider Kosovo to be part of its territory and has refused to recognize the independence it declared in 2008. Kosovo aspires to join the European Union and the United Nations. This has not been possible because its independence is not recognized by several EU member states and some major world powers on the UN Security Council.

***

Challenges for Emelia concerned employment, housing, transportation, language, and finances. And living independently.

Two weeks before she was due to vacate her college dorm in America, she secured a short-term, funded position. Her first job title was information and outreach officer for a non-governmental organization. The NGO offer was enough incentive for her to make the international move.

Her employer found housing for her, though she was responsible for paying the rent. The room was in a brick Communist-era building. Her new colleagues were quite proud of the location, within walking distance of the office as well as nightclubs, though she cared little about the latter. The lodging was convenient aside from rotating electricity outages, but everyone experienced that because the power-generating and manufacturing infrastructure had been crippled in the war. Then she started to break out in an itchy skin rash and developed painful, infected boils. Her colleagues surmised that bedbugs were the culprit and said she should leave that apartment. They set up a house-sitting arrangement for her on the edges of Pristina, from where she still had to walk to work.

The owners at her new place were an older couple planning an extended trip out of the country. Unfortunately, the couple didn't leave on the intended vacation but stayed home and followed Emelia around mercilessly any time she was home. Atypical Kosovars, they were not comfortable with her inviting guests into their home, not even a couple of people for her birthday.

Still recovering from her rash, she had been instructed to rinse herself in warm chamomile tea every day. Water pressure was too weak to transport hot water to her top-floor quarters (another infrastructure deficiency), so the landlady would bring a pot of hot water up to her, and she'd squat in the tub stirring chamomile flowers into the water and pouring cupfuls over her painful lesions.

The housing search began anew.

Her first job ended for the good reason that the project reached completion, and Emelia found another position. Many non-governmental organizations were active in Kosovo, offering a range of opportunities for talented, young college graduates in nonprofit sectors. For several NGOs she did work in public relations, research, and publication development. When an editorial board compromised the integrity of a major research publication she was working on, she resigned and took her skills elsewhere.

She began to consider pursing a graduate degree, perceiving benefits to furthering her education: It would improve her job effectiveness, and her new skills could cut costs for her nonprofit employer, which had been relying on external research contractors. In this endeavor, too, there were a few bumps along the way. She was accepted at an Ivy League school but after twice deferring due to job commitments, she lost her spot and applied at another university. After seven years in Kosovo, she began the program that ultimately granted her a master of science.

The advanced degree did enhance her credentials and strengthen her ability to conduct rigorous social-science research. Within a few years, she was speaking at international panel discussions. It was becoming obvious that Kosovo was her new long-term home.

Emelia has always found much to love in Kosovo. She was immediately charmed by spontaneous performances of musicians producing a violin or accordion and staging little concerts or sing-alongs on the street or in a café. Some of her favorite places are the public parks and the majestic mountains suited to all types of hiking. She appreciates the Kosovars' welcoming manner. Hosts consider themselves responsible for the entire time that guests stay with them, even if those guests are not friends. This practice dates back to *Kanun of Lekë Dukagjini*, centuries-old tribal Albanian customs regarding honor, solidarity, and hospitality extended to enemies as well as friends. In modern practice, this includes walking one's guests all the way to the edge of their property at the end of a visit. Emelia did not mention the fifteenth-century blood-feud aspect of the tradition by which families could avenge the life of a loved one as soon as the offending enemy left their land. (The practice has all but disappeared.)

Was she ever afraid as a young woman in a strange land? She says she felt most vulnerable, not in Kosovo, but on an occasion in Mumbai, India. In those days, a tourist had to carry cash or traveler's checks. She was nearly out of both, having spent four weeks in Kathmandu, Nepal and parts of India. On her last night, when she had to leave her hotel at four in the morning, she realized she did not have enough rupees for a taxi to the airport. The hotel manager arranged for a tuk-tuk and verified the destination and price. These motorized, three-wheeled rickshaws are small, open on all sides, and handy for navigating narrow, urban lanes. Emelia sat perched behind the driver, clutching her massive backpack. Along the way, the driver kept pulling over on the dark roads and making passes at her. The implication was that unless she kissed him, he might dump her there with her luggage on a dingy sidewalk where homeless people were building fires to keep warm. Finally, she rose up to her full height, summoned her outdoor voice, and hollered at him. He scooted along, taking her to the wrong airport, the closest one. Again, she had to insist he fulfill the commitment he had made at the hotel.

Emelia met her challenges abroad head-on with youthful energy and aptitude. She changed jobs and apartments, negotiated big cities and country roads, dealt with bureaucracies and met daily needs, made friends, and walked or rode a bicycle everywhere she went. Along the way, she mastered the complex Albanian language and learned some Serbian as well.

Through all of her adventures, she was never tempted to quit and return to the USA. The only time she felt homesick, she said, was if a family member became ill and she was too far away to visit. The rapid passage of time made her realize the opportunity costs of an engrossing overseas career.

Asked if she was optimistic about European Union accession, Emelia admitted that big challenges remained. Meanwhile, she and her colleagues continued working toward the standards that would be upheld if Kosovo were an EU member. For example, some newer laws are helping to improve living conditions. Emelia noted that a great deal can be accomplished in a smaller country, especially on the local level, where everyone knows everyone else. She's always been an optimist who asks, "What can I change today?"

YEARS LATER

Fifteen years after meeting Emelia in the USA, I had the opportunity to spend a summer working with her in Kosovo through the Fulbright Specialist Program. I got reacquainted with this American woman who still walked forty-five minutes across a park to get to work, and rode her six-speed folding bicycle everywhere else. As is generally the case in Europe, she could even take her bike on the city bus and on an airplane. She frequently did so.

By this time, Emelia's Albanian was fluent, her devotion to the nascent democracy obviously enduring, and her contributions to its society widely recognized. Still, the country awaited statehood and continued to face many of the challenges Emelia had previously made me aware of.

During my short stint of consulting in Pristina, I enjoyed a bright, clean, lovely apartment in a convenient location near downtown. The kitchen was small but adequate. The bathroom had white tile and modern fixtures. But you couldn't flush any bathroom tissue down the toilet. No one told me explicitly what to do with it. There were no residential garbage-collection services and few public trash receptacles. Getting rid of this "refuse" became a black-ops activity of stealthily finding garbage dumpsters, some of which reeked badly. Walking to work or shopping, I routinely passed through an alley where an old car was rusting away, its windows broken, and the whole vehicle stuffed with trash. Sanitation problems were not unique to this apartment or to Kosovo but prevalent throughout the region. This is part of what we mean when we talk about developing countries.

Near my apartment is Mother Teresa Boulevard, a mile-and-a-half of walking zone featuring a lively café culture. Few activities are more pleasant than to sit at a European sidewalk restaurant amid historic architecture and colorful flowers. Soak in local culture by people-watching in the open air. Well dressed professionals bustle off to work. Tourists relax. A child drops an ice cream cone and cries.

Every afternoon my colleagues took a short break without leaving the office.

"Who wants coffee?"

It was an easy habit to get into, because it cost only fifty euro cents which, for me, was practically nothing. We'd all place our copper-alloy coins on a table, and shortly thereafter a waiter would walk across the street and enter our offices with a tray full of little cups of macchiato with a frothy swirl on top. My colleague Luljeta made an observation that was only half joking: "Kosovo coffee is the best in the world, because the person who makes it has a bachelor's degree."

The larger cities boast modern architecture and medical clinics, where I received expert care twice. The countryside is breathtaking. Encompassing mountains and plains, it's about 90 percent lush forest and farmland. My husband joined me in the fall so he could hike in Kosovo and Albania. In Pristina we visited the Great Mosque and the Cathedral of Saint Mother Teresa. In front of a bookstore near the main square in Pristina was a bronze statue memorializing the diminutive founder of the Missionaries of Charity. Her presence there pays homage to her faith, good works on behalf of the poor and, not insignificantly, to her Albanian heritage.

This population has a Muslim-influenced history dating back to the Ottoman Empire. Yet I never met anyone there who attended worship services or took work breaks for daily prayers. Some Kosovars observed Ramadan. A few engaged in the thirty days of fasting. A few more celebrated Eid al-Fitr, a festive time that marks the end of the holy month.

On a free Saturday-morning tour, a city guide told us that Albanianism was the true religion of most Kosovars (especially those with Albanian roots).

At the end of my Kosovo summer, I was interviewed by a television journalist whom John had met while hiking. She asked which of the forty countries I'd visited did I like best. I tried being diplomatic, evasive, but she pressed for an answer. It would be hard to come up with category favorites let alone a single, overall preference. Finally, I adapted my father-in-law's response about favorite foods: the best meal he'd ever had was the one he'd enjoyed most recently.

THE ADVENTUROUS SEEK US

FATE HAS OTHER PLANS

"Mann tracht, und Gott lacht." *

We always wanted to be grandparents without becoming parents. Could we skip the trials of diapers, orthodontics, and teen rebellions, and fast-forward to the rewarding pride and joy of playing with grandbabies?

Finding that less than feasible, we contented ourselves with glimpses into the lives of our families' and friends' offspring.

There's nothing more heart-robbing than the unvarnished adoration of a three-year-old. To see a toddler brighten when you enter the room and run toward you, arms outspread, shrieking his nickname for you, "Ni-Ni!" Or using character voices to read to a two-year-old and hearing her announce in toddler grammar, "You funny, Unco' John!" Nothing is more humbling than sneaking a fresh strawberry when you think you're alone in the kitchen and hearing a wee voice from behind you declare, "I like *gobbie stoo!*"

As childless adults, we gather up such moments like pearls added to our growing string of treasured anecdotes, sometimes finding that the parents have forgotten their charming cuteness. One great thing in telling stories about other people's children is that it doesn't make you look boastful.

When John and I arrived at the college campus where our midlife crises had taken us, I was eager to continue interacting with young people. Cultural opportunities were abundant: live theater and poetry readings. Concerts and Old Town art walks. Guest lectures and office parties. A priority on my calendar was the fall-semester open house for international students. Having spent a decade in Europe, we welcomed the chance to socialize with people from abroad.

The mixer event at the student union buzzed with a dozen foreign accents. Young people from Germany, France, and Vietnam. From Japan, India, and Nepal. Nametags, hors d'oeuvres, and a round of short conversations prompted by cliché questions. Where did you learn such good English? Why did you choose this college? What do your parents think about your coming here? How are you feeling about America so far?

Let's get involved; let's host a student, I enthused. John was more reserved. The professorship represented a major career change. This was a new job, a new campus, a new set of colleagues. Let's not sign up yet, he advised. Wait 'til next semester or next year. We mingled and munched on appetizers, then signed the guest book but did not register for a match-up.

A week later, the Friendship Family director contacted us to say that the friendly little Vietnamese gal who had greeted us at the sign-in table was requesting that John and I become her host family.

What are you going to say when Fate calls upon you in such an obvious and adorable way?

But what did we have to offer a young visitor? No children or extended family to help entertain her. No grand holiday traditions. No engaging hobbies. No exotic cooking skills. Not even a regular meal schedule. The program matchmaker advised that we didn't need to do a lot of special things with our new friend. Simply welcome her to our home once or twice a month to join us for whatever we might be doing that weekend.

We would go for a drive or short hike, or take LoAn shopping because, like most foreign students, she didn't have a car. Before long, I was baking chocolate chip cookies while LoAn was cooking hunks of beef in our kitchen. She washed dishes one at a time with a rag instead of filling the big double sink with hot water. One afternoon, she stood in our kitchen with the fridge door open, pondering what to snack on. Reacting more like a grandmother than a mom, I thrilled at seeing her make herself at home. A happy little tingling ran up and down my arms, and there was no way I was going to say, "Don't stand there with the refrigerator open."

As a testament to how well she learned our peccadilloes, such as John's irregular hours and my regular nagging, LoAn began to keep tabs on him for me. "Martine," she tattled one evening. "John's drinking Mountain Dew after 5 o'clock!"

When she went on a short class-related trip, she phoned us the first evening. The call startled me a little. "Is everything OK?" I asked. "Oh, yes," she replied. "In my family, we always call one another at the end of our travel, to let our parents know we've arrived safely. So I wanted to call someone."

We couldn't help but fall in love with this beautiful, tiny, black-haired girl.

Before she met us, LoAn had already had more housing adventures than any 17-year-old visitor should experience. She was the first child in her family to study abroad. Not waiting until college, she had come to America her senior year of high school with an exchange program in Mississippi. The program placed students in local homes to live full time for a schoolyear. Host families were typically professors, teachers, church members, civic leaders. LoAn's particular arrangement surprised her a bit, but she didn't complain. Her host was a single mother working part time at a fast-food restaurant and living in a small trailer. Having limited transportation, she was struggling to work and feed her own two kids. Almost immediately she began to rely on LoAn to provide childcare.

After a few months, the high school principal became aware of where LoAn was living and asked her about the conditions. She admitted to him that it might be less than ideal. The host's sister was a prostitute, and the woman had hoped that getting involved in a student exchange program might enhance her reputation in the community. The principal said he'd find LoAn another place to live and ultimately had her move in with him and his wife for the rest of the year.

College housing presented its own pitfalls. In the interest of being thrifty, LoAn did as many international scholars do in the USA. She shared a small apartment with several other students, sometimes people she barely knew. One weekend a new roommate asked if LoAn would ride with her to Boise. The big city. After several hours of driving, they would share a room. When they got to the Idaho capital, the other young woman hooked up with some guy she'd just met and brought him in to share the motel room. It was an awkward situation for our young friend, but she managed to fall asleep. In the middle of the night, the man and woman awakened her and suggested, "Wouldn't you like to go to breakfast?" She was confused. They repeated the question. "Why don't you go out for breakfast now?" In other words, they wanted the room – and the bed – to themselves and were proposing that LoAn leave at 3 in the morning. With no car. No credit card. Nowhere to go. She called us. John was furious and ready to jump in his car, go rescue our friend, and give the other two individuals a swift kick in the pants. Not necessarily in that order. I was inclined to report the other student to campus authorities, but apparently you can't get someone expelled for being self-centered and reckless.

Having spent her young life working on her education to improve her prospects in life, LoAn soon realized that our little college was not academically challenging enough. Thinking of transferring elsewhere, she decided to visit her parents before making a change. At the end of spring semester, she moved out of her apartment and into our house for a few days. We brought a carload of clothing, books, and kitchenware from her place to ours so she could quit paying rent and take her time packing. Among the items she wanted to take home were multiple big bottles of over-the-counter medicines and nutritional supplements.

Medicines are readily available at Vietnamese pharmacies, LoAn said, but you don't always know what you're getting.

When I went upstairs on the morning of her departure, her luggage appeared to be ready to go. When I peeked in an hour later, the contents of both of her suitcases were scattered about the floor, as she started over. Watching the clock and considering her upcoming deadline, I grew nervous. She kept packing and unpacking. Finally, I implored John: "She's your kid; you go help her!"

He drove her to the little local airport but came dashing back alone twenty minutes later, frantically looking for another bag. The suitcases were too heavy, and the contents had to be split up. Off he went again, and I imagine that the fastidious packing of that afternoon gave way to a rush of cramming and stuffing personal belongings into new configurations under the prying eyes of bemused strangers in the terminal.

Weeks later LoAn came back from Vietnam carrying jars of fish oil and pork lard wrapped in layers of cloth, and multi-part steel steamer pots that we couldn't pry apart without using hot- and cold-water tactics. LoAn was vexed that her special spicy pork sausage had been confiscated by Customs agents. Don't you always wonder if they immediately dump your precious contraband into the garbage or eat the good stuff on their lunch break? And which scenario would make you feel worse?

She brought us all kinds of undeserved presents. Scarves and table linens. From one of her suitcases emerged an 18-inch decorative plate. It was painted with a scene of a man in a sunhat working a rice field with a water buffalo against a backdrop of streams, foot bridges, and mountains. That heavy porcelain plate has hung on a wall of our home no matter where we've lived ever since then.

When our young friend decided to transfer to a larger university in another state, we were sad but suitably impressed with her ambition and the research she had done to make it possible. LoAn would be moving from our little open-enrollment school to the more prestigious University of Texas at Austin. She'd figured out how she could afford the tuition. She knew the curriculum would be more stimulating and her credentials more notable. When she consulted us on her course load, we were concerned. This was a harder school; should she really take six classes her first semester there? "The first four classes are just math," she reassured us, "so that part is easy."

She wanted to major in mathematics, but her father told her that computer science would be more practical. Preparing to meet him, we considered helping her make the case for her first academic choice, but when we saw his determination, we quickly backed off. After she graduated, she would be much sought after by multinational asset-management firms in New York City. Big-name companies that hired young Asians, who lived crammed into pricey apartments, and worked eighty hours a week.

So off she went to seek her Fortune 500. Lovely LoAn was breaking our hearts. In the good way.

* *Man plans, and God laughs.*

⸺ ! ⸺

A LESSON IN RECIPROCITY

Our next foreign-student experience was multi-faceted. Tanisha had come to the USA to complete a master's degree in environmental engineering. Her intention was to return to Nepal and contribute to ecologically efficient energy production there. She was homesick and lonely, far from her closeknit family of six siblings.

As with LoAn the year before, the experiences my husband and I offered at our friendship-family meetings with Tanisha were pleasant but unspectacular. We would sometimes cook together. She went with us to a Christmas piano singalong at the home of the university's athletic director. We gave her rides to the grocery store. On one such outing I gave her some small thing: ink pens or sticky notes, I think. She reached into her purse and came up with a little pink hair clip to give me. That should have clued me in to the importance of reciprocity in her culture.

A year after Tanisha arrived, her younger sister, Kalyani, came to begin undergraduate studies. We were willing to expand our hosting duties to include her, but Tanisha announced that her sister should get her own host family. She was teasing. I think.

The two scholars shared a small apartment near campus. They also shared a laptop computer, one cellphone, and a bicycle. To further economize, they accepted another roommate, a redhaired American girl who left inspirational quotes on the walls and fridge. Unfortunately, she liked to bake cookies much more than she liked to wash cookie sheets or buy her share of the bathroom tissue.

How do international students choose a college in America? Most would like to consider academic programs and location. Many, however, have to look first at affordability.

"How did you find our little college town on the map?"

"We looked for the lowest fees and costs of living."

Funny, that, since local students complained how expensive school was. American girls were driving new cars and eating fast food, having their hair dyed multiple colors, getting acrylic fingernails, and replacing iPhones accidentally flushed down public toilets. Not so, international students. Foreign families sometimes borrowed money to make their bank accounts look flush for the financial qualification part of the application process. After acceptance, they passed the money along to another family to do the same. These students had entry visas that permitted them to take jobs only on campus, generally twenty hours a week, while they were required to carry full-time academic course loads. They borrowed or shared textbooks or used reference materials at the library.

In the third year another sister, Kirti, came to start college too. Now three sisters were sharing one bedroom, one computer and one phone. That's how they managed. And they didn't complain.

Their life stories impressed us, evoking admiration, fondness, and concern. We basked in their friendliness, their photos from home, and their native dances performed in colorful costume: red skirts with wide sashes wrapped multiple times around the midriff. We loved being involved; we wanted to be helpful. Because our financial status was so secure and comfortable in contrast to their more challenging conditions, we occasionally sought to ease their burden. Could we buy them a bicycle or computer? *No, thank you.*

When sister number three was hit by a car while riding her bike to campus to register for her first college classes, no student insurance coverage was yet in effect for the bureaucratic reason that the schoolyear had not officially begun. We found Kirti a physical therapist and offered to cover medical expenses. That would not be necessary, the girls informed us in a tersely worded, handwritten letter. "We have our own parents." It seems we had gone too far.

As Tanisha neared graduation, her parents began talking about marriage and how they wanted to decide on a husband for her, in accordance with tradition. "You would have the right to choose among several proposed matches, to say no to a particular suitor," her mother assured her. "Yes, Mother, but that kind of choice is not real choice," Tanisha insisted.

A year later she married an American engineering student at city hall, a ceremony that had to be repeated with Nepalese blessings in order for the extended family back home to consider the union legitimate. Later there would be a more elaborate wedding celebration in the bride's village in the Himalayan foothills.

What do parents expect when they send their 18-year-old daughters to the United States? They taste adventures and new freedoms. They are at the age when young people are beginning to see themselves as adults and to develop an interest in starting their own families and households. They are intelligent and pretty; they're talented and have charming accents. It's not surprising that they attract romantic as well as professional proposals while they are here.

Like so many graduate students from other countries who fall in love with a job or a lifestyle or a man, Tanisha stayed in America. She completed doctoral research into using biological matrices to produce electricity, but she did not return to Nepal to apply her knowledge there. The brain drain must be palpable in some of these developing nations. What becomes of the goal of bringing clean energy back to the home country? Of solving clean-water problems and food shortages or treating the sick?

Does the sense of community responsibility get lost in pursuit of American individualism?

⁓ I ⁓

NO COINCIDENCES

Thanh Van and I met at a podiatrist's office. In his parking lot, actually. She had an appointment, and my husband did too. Neither one could enter the clinic directly because this was during the COVID years. Following instructions on the door, John dialed the prescribed phone number and was told to wait outside until a receptionist came out and called his name. A tiny woman in what appeared to be a black wig was trying to dial the number too. Watching from the shade of a nearby tree, I had the impression her phone wasn't working. She might never get inside.

I asked if I could help. Once we got that sorted out, she joined me under the tree and began telling me I should gather some of the pods to take home and plant. John was called inside. The lady told me her feet were bothering her due to recent chemotherapy treatments.

Then she was called inside. Through a window, I could see her in the waiting room. We waved at each other.

Oh, I hope she comes back out before John does, so I can talk with her again. It was a little prayer.

She did come back out first.

"My name is Van," she said. "Maybe we can meet for coffee."

I gave her my business card and invited her to contact me.

I've done this before, and no one ever follows up.

This woman did call! She suggested we meet at Le Buzz, a café halfway between our homes. That morning, or maybe at our next meeting, she mentioned working on her memoirs but was concerned about finalizing a written manuscript in English because her native language was Vietnamese.

"This is a lucky day for you!" I said. "I'm a journalist and a teacher. If you show me what you've got so far, I'll take a look at it for you."

Being a deeply spiritual person, Thanh Van was convinced it was not mere luck that had brought us together.

She had several chapters written, so I started reading and marking up drafts. We met periodically to exchange papers. The pages of her life were replete with Bible verses. She'd been born in North Vietnam, but her family was Christian and staunchly anti-communist.

Life was hard even before her mother died and her father remarried. The new woman was the classic wicked stepmother who, once she had a baby and got a job, wielded increasing power in the family. Van's chores included carrying water from the village well and hand-washing her stepmother's underwear. She also went to school, studying mathematics and learning French.

During the Vietnam War, Thanh Van met an American government contractor and eventually came to the States to marry him, only to discover he already had a wife. Making the best of the situation, she started college and began student-teaching. Her work was primarily with foreign youths, impressing on them the importance of learning mathematics.

"Math is an international language," Thanh Van told her pupils. "It can help you get a good job anywhere." She found it satisfying to mentor cross-cultural students, pushing them in reading and math.

"Now I want to do the Ph.D.," she informed her academic advisor. "I would like to become an example to other foreign students."

"They don't need your example," the advisor rebuked her. "Your English is not good enough."

Thanh Van was stunned but not deterred. She competed the advanced degree and became a curriculum developer as well as an instructor. She got married too.

After retiring, she contributed to the success of her sister's new company. She worked even after she got liver cancer, a condition she said was not unusual for people from Vietnam. She continued working for her siblings after her husband died. As a volunteer, Thanh Van visited cancer patients in hospitals, encouraging them to believe they would survive as she had. This continued until she was diagnosed with cancer again. Pancreatic cancer this time. When she began chemotherapy treatments, she was no longer qualified to make official calls referring to herself as a survivor.

It was about that time that she and I met.

She shared coffee and homemade *pho*, and offered cacti from her garden. She called when she felt up to going for a walk in Tohono Chul botanical gardens. Or when she didn't feel so strong and would welcome a short visit.

She lived an impressive number of years with her disease, thanks to multiple interventions and perhaps a strong will and faith. When someone you love is chronically ill and keeps surviving health crises over a period of years, you begin to think he or she is invincible.

But time and cancer march inexorably.

We both felt the pressure of an impending deadline, and Thanh Van delivered her manuscript to a publisher while she was still able to sell and sign copies of her book.

Offering her favorite niece some advance instructions on a funeral and eulogy, she said, "Tell people about my book. But don't tell them too much; I still want them to buy it."

※

FROM RUSSIA FOR LOVE

Ekaterina had been happily married in Nakhodka, but after her husband died, she struggled to regain her footing. After a few years, a friend suggested she attend an event where Russian women could be paired with American men, who would marry them and take them to start a new life in the USA. Two of her daughters were old enough to stay behind, but she took the youngest girl with her.

Ekaterina found herself on the long road to Oregon and, hopefully, toward citizenship. Her new husband took her to a remote homestead, where she soon developed misgivings about the man's intentions toward her preschool daughter. Ekaterina divorced the man, but the separation put her visa status in jeopardy. She married someone else, based on misguided legal advice, and was subsequently told that this marriage further reduced her chances of attaining U.S. citizenship. She divorced again.

As a single mother, she hoped to work in accounting, for which she had been trained in Russia. Instead, she toiled for decades as a housekeeper, earning no retirement or health benefits. Meanwhile her youngest daughter grew up in American schools, forgetting her native Russian language.

Years went by. One day Ekaterina was stopped for a driving violation, and the police officer moved to arrest her. Thinking to evade U.S. courts, she protested that she had a right to embassy protection.

Mistake.

That admission put her into the U.S. Immigration system, where she sought various means of remaining in America. She wanted to stay in this country for the sake of her foreign-born daughter, who was by this time about to finish high school. This predicament led to Ekaterina's hiring of expensive specialist attorneys who ultimately could not save her from deportation. Neither could they guarantee her daughter's status. The child might be able to stay in America without her mother or any other family. Or she might be deported to her birthplace, whose language and culture were completely foreign to her.

As Ekaterina grew more discouraged and disillusioned, her attitude toward the USA took on an acerbic edge. Her allegiance to her birthplace reemerged. She began to speak of Russia as "home" again, the land where she belonged. A place where she would see family members and meet her new grandbaby. Where she could get health care for free and a small stipend to live on.

By the end of that year, she returned – was returned – to her homeland, a country that was by now strange to her. Her daughter remained in limbo in the USA.

FIN

GLOSSARY

Following are informal descriptions of some foreign-languages or unusual words used in the context of this book. They are not intended as comprehensive definitions. Due to transliteration from Arabic into English, spellings vary.

Abaya. Cloak-like outer garment worn by some Muslim women in the Middle East. It covers from neck to ankles and has long sleeves. Traditionally black, but color variations are increasing in popularity.

Apostille. Certificate authenticating an official public document for international use in countries that are part of the 1961 Hague Convention. Other countries use a similar process.

Baksheesh. Gift, tip, or gratuity. Commonly used in parts of the Middle East and northern Africa.

Burkini. Full-coverage swimsuit favored by some Muslim women for modesty while swimming. A portmanteau of "burqa" and "bikini."

Burqa or battoulah. Bedouin mask covering part of a woman's nose and mouth. It resembles a large mustache. Made of fabric with a metallic-looking finish patterned with intricate designs. Its usage is decreasing, but it is sometimes worn by older women for special occasions. In the social context in this book, it does *not* refer to the heavy, full head covering that leaves only a mesh screen to see through.

Dishdasha, djellaba, thobe. Traditional, long robes worn by many men in the Middle East and northern Africa. Names, styles, and colors vary by region.

Felucca. Traditional wooden sailboat featuring large, triangular sails. Used on the Nile River for fishing, transport, and tourist rides near Aswan and Luxor in Egypt.

Fête du mouton or Eid al-Adha. Islamic Festival of Sacrifice commemorating Prophet Abraham's willingness to surrender his son as an act of obedience to God. Celebrated at the end of the annual Hajj pilgrimage to Mecca.

Garrab. Traditional Moroccan water sellers, known for distinctive red costumes and ornate hats. They offer refreshment from brass cups in hot public places.

Insha'Allah. If God so wills. A reminder that nothing can occur outside the will of God, and nothing should be taken for granted.

Jahreswagen. A German automobile less than a year old, in excellent condition. May come from a company fleet or lease return.

Kandura. Traditional long, white Emirati man's robe featuring a silk-threaded *sharaba* tassel. (Similar to dishdasha, djellaba, thobe.)

Luqaimat. Crisp, deep-fried dough ball soaked in honey or syrup. An Emirati dessert.

Majboos (or machboos) chicken. Aromatic Middle Eastern dish featuring spiced chicken and fragrant basmati rice. Popular in the Arabian Gulf.

Mastaba. Flat-topped rectangular tomb constructed from mud-brick or stone in ancient Egypt.

Milcha. Formal, legal marriage contract signing attended by a few close family members. In Arabic cultures, it commonly precedes large celebrations by several months.

Muezzin. Muslim official who calls believers to prayer five times a day from a mosque's minaret, often using a loudspeaker.

NGO or non-governmental organization. An entity operating independently from government control, usually nonprofit and focused on issues such as human rights, health, and environment. Often funded by government grants, corporate donations, and private-sector contributions.

Niqab. Traditional veil covering the lower part of the face (nose to neck). Typically made of black, soft, breathable fabric. Now worn by a minority of women in the UAE.

Salwar kameez. Loose tunic and baggy, pleated trousers often worn by men in Afghanistan and Pakistan.

Shayla. Long, rectangular headscarf worn by many Muslim women to cover their hair. In the UAE, it is draped simply, leaving the face uncovered. Traditionally black.

Vada pav. Popular vegetarian Indian street food in Maharashtra, consisting of potato dumpling rolled in spiced gram (chickpea) flour batter and deep-fried. Served on bread, often with green chutney and garlic.

***

UAE. The United Arab Emirates. A federation of seven emirates that became an independent country on December 2, 1971. This followed a 1968 announcement that the United Kingdom intended to withdraw from the Trucial States, which it had considered a protectorate since 1820. The UAE consists of 32,300 square miles (83,600 square kilometers) situated on the Arabian Gulf (or Persian Gulf) bordering Oman and Saudi Arabia. Its land is rich in minerals. The federated entities, originally united under the leadership of Sheikh Zayed bin Sultan Al Nahyan, are: Abu Dhabi (largest and the nation's capital), Dubai, Sharjah, Ajman, Fujairah, Umm Al Quwain, and Ras Al Khaimah. Population: about 11 million, of whom about 1.2 million are Emirati.

***

MISFITS FURTHER ABROAD

DISCUSSION GUIDE

1. Which location discussed in this book most intrigues you?
2. The vignettes in *Misfits Further Abroad* describe a range of cultural contexts. In which ways might your actions in such situations be similar? How might you react differently?
3. Are the writer's fears normal or out of proportion with the risks faced?
4. What is unique about the author's voice or tone?
5. The author states that excursions can take visitors, not just to another place, but to another time. What does she mean?
6. Does the writer treat her subjects fairly and objectively, avoiding stereotypes?
7. To what extent would you be inclined to obey all the laws and customs of the places you visit?
8. What are some positive ways to interact with people who have religious beliefs that do not align with yours?
9. What was the most surprising or interesting custom portrayed in this book?
10. What is your reaction to the manner of choosing marriage partners exemplified in these stories? The book describes garments worn by people in some foreign settings. What is your perspective on these styles of dress?
11. What value might there be in revisiting past wars?
12. What age would you consider the best for traveling abroad?
13. What is the difference between touring and traveling?
14. Does traveling abroad or reading about international cultures change your reaction to the range of languages and cultures found in your own country? How so?

AUTHOR'S BIOGRAPHY

MARTINE ROBINSON BEACHBOARD

The author has always been fascinated by languages, cultures, and travel. She has lived in or visited forty countries and served as a Fulbright Scholar in Kosovo. In her first career, she was a newspaper editor. Her weekly personal column developed a loyal following and evoked a range of reader responses and emotions.

She was awarded first place in column writing from the Arizona Press Club. Her editing was recognized with top honors four times by Arizona Press Women. A Penney-Missouri Newspaper Awards competition named her a finalist in single-story reporting.

Early in her journalism career, she learned that everyone had a story. With increased interviewing experience, she realized that everyone *was* a story. When life and work took her overseas, she continued writing about the surprising situations and quirky characters she encountered there.

Her first collection of people stories was released in book form by Livingwell Publications as *Misfits Abroad: Adventures in Love, Language, and Foreign Lands* in 2024. While its vignettes centered on Europe, the current work takes readers to Asia, the Middle East, and beyond.

A former professor, Martine Robinson Beachboard is a teacher of English as a Second Language and a reading tutor for primary-school children.

***

AUTHOR'S NOTE

Thank you for spending time with *Misfits*. We hope you enjoyed the book and will share it with other readers. The author would be appreciative if you posted an online review:

> Review on Amazon: https://shorturl.at/87mjI
> Review on Goodreads: https://shorturl.at/cjdgJ

You may contact Martine Robinson Beachboard through her website at:

> https://mrbeachboard.com/my-new-book/

Books by this author:

Misfits Abroad: Adventures in Love, Language, and Foreign Lands
Misfits Further Abroad: People and Adventures Around the World

***

www.ingramcontent.com/pod-product-compliance
Lightning Source LLC
LaVergne TN
LVHW010318070526
838199LV00065B/5601